15
minute
parenting
8-12 YEARS

BOOKS BY JOANNA FORTUNE

15-Minute Parenting 0–7 Years
15-Minute Parenting 8–12 Years

JOANNA FORTUNE

15

minute
parenting
8-12 YEARS

Published by Thread in 2020

An imprint of Storyfire Ltd.
Carmelite House
50 Victoria Embankment
London EC4Y 0DZ

www.thread-books.com

ISBN: 978-1-83888-627-1
eBook ISBN: 978-1-83888-626-4

The information contained in this book is not advice and the
method may not be suitable for everyone to follow. This book is not
intended to replace the services of trained professionals or to be a
substitute for medical advice. You are advised to consult a doctor on
any matters relating to your child's or your health, and in particular
on any matters that may require diagnosis or medical attention.

For all of the children who so generously share their inner world with me and from whom I continue to learn so much.

Joanna Fortune (MICP; MIFPP; Reg Pract APPI; CTTTS; ApSup PTI) is an accredited clinical psychotherapist and attachment specialist. She founded the Solamh Parent Child Relationship Clinic in Dublin in 2010 (www.solamh.com) where she works with families around a variety of issues. She is a recognised supervisor, trainer and conference speaker in her field. In 2017, she delivered a TEDx Talk on the topic 'Social media – the ultimate shame game?' Having previously written a parenting column for *The Sunday Times* (Ireland Edition) she continues to write and contribute to articles on child development and parenting in various other print publications. She is also a regular media contributor to a variety of national radio and TV shows, and the parenting consultant on the weekly parenting slot on Newstalk FM's award-winning *Moncrieff show*.

CONTENTS

INTRODUCTION

15-Minute Parenting – The Small Changes That Make Big Differences

If you haven't read book one in this series let me talk you through my 15-Minute Parenting model. I am not for one moment suggesting that all you need to do is spend 15 minutes parenting your children during a given day (wouldn't that be something?) but I am stating that if you devote 15 mindfully present play-based minutes to your child(ren) each day, you will quickly see positive changes in your relationship with them. This is a model based on fewer tears and more laughter, where small changes really do make big differences.

I am Joanna Fortune, a psychotherapist who specialises in the parent–child relationship from the cradle to the rave, i.e. from pregnancy right up to young adulthood. I have worked in private clinical practice for 10 years and before this for 12 years in the non-governmental organisation sector in Ireland. I have worked with hundreds of families across thousands of clinical hours over the span of my career and have progressed to training and supervising other therapists in how to do this work. My 15-Minute Parenting model is the result of all of these hours with all kinds of families in a variety of settings from a variety of backgrounds. In my experience, and with very rare exception, most parents are doing the very best that they can and, again with very rare exception, everyone can (re)learn to play and to develop a play-based therapeutic approach to parenting. In my 20 years of clinical practice the most common phrase I hear from parents is that after they've done a day's work, collected their children from childcare and got home to put dinner on the table, they feel lucky if they have 15 minutes a day to spend with their children before it is time for bed. They ask, 'What can I do in just 15 minutes a day?' and my answer is, 'Plenty, and most definitely enough.'

Some of us will experience challenges in our parent–child relationship that certainly cannot be addressed or resolved using this model alone and will require the input of a suitably qualified mental-health professional. However, many more of us can experience more mild to moderate level challenges as our children grow and develop and as our parenting journey grows and develops with them, and this is where my 15-Minute Parenting model is most effective. Even if you are not experiencing challenges in your relationship with your child, there is no such thing as too much play, and there is always benefit to be had by increasing and sustaining the level of playfulness in our relationships with our children, each other and also with ourselves. My model is based on the premise that play isn't a set of activities or games alone but more a state of mind and a way of being. There are benefits in this for all of us in terms of our mental well-being. Always make time and find opportunities for play!

In book one of this series I focused on introducing the model, early child development theory and how to apply my model with children aged 0–7 years old. This second book in the series looks closer at middle childhood, that 8–12-year-old bracket, and the third book will take you through those teenage years. What you will discover in these books is a road map for playful connection and how to learn and use the language of play to strengthen and enhance your relationship with your child.

I'll show you how you can apply therapeutic play (including some techniques that you do not need to be a therapist to do) to your parenting toolkit in a way that will enable you to better understand your relationship with your children as they grow and develop, and ensure that your parenting is growing and developing with them.

Middle childhood, the period for those aged 8–12 years old, is often the most overlooked and under-discussed phase of children's development. We talk extensively about the all-important early years and then how to negotiate the challenging teenage years, but middle childhood is often a forgotten space. This is a great shame, as understanding what is going on for your child in their middle-childhood phase of development actually helps secure the groundwork for what you will need to do when adolescence does come knocking.

These middle childhood years are a time for significant growth and development across cognitive, social, emotional and especially physical faculties. Your child's brain is evolving and becoming more refined. It does this through a process called *synaptic pruning*, which simply put means that your child's brain is cutting back on extra synapses to ensure more efficient brain functioning. This allows for more complex information to be taken in and processed as our brains continue to mature into adulthood. Synaptic pruning is an essential phase of middle-childhood development and the environment in which your child is growing up. This is a sensitive stage of child development precisely because of the active role that environmental (i.e. physical environment and psychosocial and emotional environment) has on brain development. Your 8–12-year-old's brain is in a constant state of flux and their daily experiences are the fodder for this development.

In book one (0–7 years), I talked you through the role of play in those early formative years and now you will read about how play remains an essential part of this stage of development too. Play is the means to creating the types of daily experiences your child needs to enable important brain changes. It is precisely through play that children learn how to engage and interact with the world and people around them. Play is crucial for healthy brain development at all stages of development because it sets children up to activate their creativity through developing imagination. They learn that they have a desire and free will of their own, which helps build emotional resilience, and they acquire the physical dexterity, flexibility and coordination that support their cognitive development too.

Play continues to serve an important role in children's emotional development during middle childhood. When they are afforded the opportunity – and indeed encouraged by their parents and important caregivers – to engage in physical and imaginative play, children of this age (8–12 years) gravitate towards physical and imaginative play as much as they do screen-based play. Children who engage in physical (outdoor as well) and imaginative play associate this play with effecting strong positive emotions; not being able to engage in this kind of play is associated with more negative emotions, including anxiety-based symptoms.

However, this is also an age when we are most likely to stop playing *with* our children. We may deem them to have outgrown 'play' and we stop talking to them about magic and imagination. We tend to see our children at this age withdraw from active play into more passive play experiences like gaming or screen-based play. What follows in these chapters is a breakdown of the neurological, physical and emotional development of this age group and how you can keep play alive in your relationship with your child throughout these years.

'BUT WHY, BUT WHY, BUT WHY???'

At eight years old your child is having a significant growth spurt – physically, emotionally and cognitively. From a parenting point of view, children reach peak question asking at this age. When they are discovering something new they will ask a seemingly endless list of questions that will stretch you to the very depths of your own knowledge limits. However, rest assured that this isn't an attempt to catch you out but rather their way of gathering enough information to begin to draw their own conclusions about what they are learning. It is the beginning of a new learning pattern, and those questions and wonderings are to be encouraged. You can be playful in your responses and when you don't know, say you don't know. You can pause and say, 'What a great question. I don't know the answer but how about we work it out together' and do some book/online/active experiential working it out together for shared learning. You can also try reflecting to deepen their emotional reflection on their quest for knowledge. Try saying something like, 'You're really curious about this. I wonder what it is that's so interesting for you about it.' By 'wondering' you are bringing them deeper into their own reflective process. They are beginning to grow into more mature children (a gradual process that doesn't happen overnight!) and this transition makes this a really interesting age for both parents and children.

IF THEY SEE IT THEY CAN BE IT – LEAD BY POSITIVE EXAMPLE

In terms of the physical growth, it is really more about refinement than major development, and it is around this age that they begin to lose their 'young child' look and take on that so called 'big boy/girl' appearance, although puberty may still be a way off for them. This is a key age for children to decide whether or not they are into sports. Maintaining regular physical activity has multiple benefits as they continue to grow and develop even beyond the physical. It is linked to confidence. If they see their parents being active and invested in physical activity it can also help, as *if they see it, they can be it*, right?

It is also around eight years old when body talk becomes more of a conversation point. You might notice that your eight-year-old is more aware of their body – their shape, size, weight and self-confidence becomes more of a focus than previous years. They oscillate wildly between confidence and doubt during middle childhood, starting around eight years old. There is more on this in Chapter 6, but it is also a good reason to ensure that some kind of physical activity remains part of their life, allowing you to shift focus onto what their bodies can do rather than what they look like.

GROWING UP MEANS GROWING INWARDS TOO

Emotionally, your eight-year-old is probably starting to show you that they are capable of considering other people's feelings in a more meaningful way than before. When they get clothes as a gift from a relative they will be able to smile and say thank you even if they feel disappointed in the gift itself. Brace yourself for requests, or, more likely, demands for increased privacy around now too. Giving them some increased privacy, privileges and opportunities for independence does not mean acquiescing to every demand but being mindful that they tend to start pulling away from parents a little more at this stage. We need to afford them the space to do so, within our parental boundaries and limits.

You might also notice a change in how they physically interact with you. They may be more resistant to holding hands in public or giving you kisses goodbye, yet when they are emotionally distressed or worried you will find they want all of those things from you. They may well initiate when they want physical affection and may rebuff your instigating it. This is entirely healthy and normal and a part of their psychosocial development at this stage, but I would also encourage parents to keep that hugs/kisses door open and keep offering, even when they shrug you off. This communicates (in a doing rather than just saying way) to your child that you are available with affection whenever they do want that physical connection with you.

Very soon after this, within just a year for many children, you will start to see a more noticeable shift towards puberty in your child. For girls, puberty can begin anytime between eight and 12 years old; with boys it is more likely to be between nine and 14 years.

Your nine-year-old will start to demand that they have a more active say in family decisions. This should be encouraged in terms of engagement and promoting their voice BUT, and it is a big but, this needs to be managed within your parental boundaries. Find a part of the family decision they can have a say in within a boundaried choice. For example, 'We're going camping for our family holiday. We'll go to one of these two camping sites; which one would you like best?' – you are clearly happy with both options ahead of inviting them to have their say. This is also a time when you can provide opportunities for independence-building, so increase the chores and expectation that they interact with other adults in public, such as shop assistants and restaurant staff.

In spite of them asserting they know far more than you at this age, you are still their greatest influence, so heap on the praise for their efforts and maintain those gentle yet firm boundaries while they roll their eyes and sigh at your efforts to do so.

Their strong desire to fit into and be part of a peer group is very pronounced now (more on that in Chapter 2) so their susceptibility to peer pressure is also increasing. A key parenting goal during middle childhood is to invest in your child's emotional resilience and capacity to withstand these external influences. It is vital to be tuned into the media and peer influences your child is exposed to. This is a time to get interested in what they are interested in (interested is curious, not interrogating – this can feel like a finer line than it needs to be and getting the distinction correct now will greatly help when it comes to adolescence).

Your nine-year-old is capable of being reasoned with. This doesn't mean they are *reasonable* all the time, or indeed any of the time, but what it does mean is that when they get it wrong, when they lose their temper and lash out (physically perhaps but more likely a verbal lashing out), they have the capacity to reflect on what happened, take responsibility and come and make repair by saying that they are sorry. You will have been laying the ground work in the years leading up to this stage by directing, nudging and prompting them to do exactly this. At around nine years old they will start to show that they are capable of initiating this course of reflective action themselves.

Children tend to show a gendered preference in their play now, playing with children the same gender as themselves. You may also see a drop in their engagement with imaginative play and a pull towards more structured play like board games. This is fine but I would strongly advocate you persist in your 15 minutes of play a day and use structured games and activities to achieve this connection with them. I will scatter games and activities to achieve this throughout the book.

THE TWEEN YEARS

Because middle childhood is complex and less well discussed, I am breaking down each stage year by year for developmental progress so that you can track where you and your child are at. This said, bear in mind that no two children, even of the same age, develop at the same pace, so focus on the developmental age of your child rather than their chronological age. If they behave as though they are eight rather than their 10 years of age, parent them as an eight-year-old. Middle childhood is itself also fragmented into pre-tween and tween years. Between 10 and 12 are the so-called tween years.

The term *tween* actually stems from the English language preposition *between* to indicate a position in the middle of two extremes but in this context is also intended to bring to mind the fast-approaching teen years. It is a relatively new term in parenting and developmental vernacular and truly stems from marketing efforts to pre-teens (mostly girls), strengthened by establishing them as this niche group. So just as you feel you have a handle on parenting through middle childhood, you are faced with big changes again at around 10 years old.

Emotional changes are evident in both boys and girls at this age but perhaps more pronounced in girls who tend to display a more overt volatility in their moods from now on. Some children seem to become pseudo-adolescent overnight, while other 10-year-olds are still playing with their toys and looking to dress up at this age. There is nothing wrong with either behaviour pattern; it is about how quickly hormones kick off in some children over others.

So while they have developed a capacity to better understand and manage their emotional states, they now have strong mood swings that can derail them in this regard. Physically they are changing (or not – and either can be stressful) and they are trying to manage all of that physical and emotional change along with regular day-to-day stresses and expectations.

You will also observe that they are drawn to older children, teenagers in particular (in real life and those they seek to emulate from online influences and YouTubers) so expect a shift in attitude about what clothes they will wear, how they want to style their hair and the type of music they choose to listen to. Encourage this expression and exploration phase as best you can, within your parental boundaries. Purple hair may not be appropriate for school but perhaps a temporary spray-on colour can be allowed during school holidays. Similarly, a certain type of dress may be expected at school and family events, but perhaps in free weekend time they can choose their own outfits. You are avoiding unnecessary conflict but maintaining boundaries. It's a case of not 'no' so much as 'not now'.

In this early tween stage they are still in that age of parental command when they may well resist your authority but can accept that you are in charge.

Cognitively, your 10-year-old tween is showing themselves capable of more complex thoughts and formulating a detailed opinion on things. This is a great time to get to know who they are becoming. Invite them to join in with conversations about world events, things happening in your locality and community. Playfully engage them by wondering what decisions they would make if they were a world leader of a given country featuring in the news. Invite their opinions on all matters and encourage them to substantiate their opinions as they express them by gently bringing them deeper into the thinking and feeling process: 'Oh that is an interesting way to think about it. I wonder why you think X would be a good solution to this problem and what else might need to happen?'

Material your child is expected to master in school also shifts up a gear at this age and it is not uncommon for struggles in certain subjects to emerge here. Keep focusing on praising effort over outcome and don't dismiss their struggles or disappointment but rather model empathy and acceptance while then bringing the focus back to effort they have put in. Celebrate failure as an opportunity to learn.

Developmentally, 10-year-olds still show a keen interest in playing and enjoy team sports as well as individual activities such as cycling, skating, roller skating, scooters and so on – things that require increased skill and effort to achieve mastery over the task.

Of course, it is also an age when they really enjoy gadgets and screen- and digital-based devices. I am not saying no to this but I am saying not only this. If your child enjoys experimenting with digital devices and time on YouTube, meet them in this interest. Give them use of your digital camera and invite them to pick a theme (or you assign one) and say that you will both take images and videos on this theme for one to two weeks and then will put them together as a digital collage and share it with each other, making a story out of it.

GAMES TO KEEP YOU IN SYNC – OR GET YOU BACK IN SYNC – WITH YOUR CHILD

Ensure that you keep your 15 minutes of play each day active here by using some of these activities that tweens respond to.

Games like **We went on a picnic** whereby each player says in turn *'We went on a picnic and we brought _____'* (say a food or play item like cheese/eggs/a frisbee/a beach ball, etc.). Each player repeats what has been said before him or her and adds an item on. You can go as long as possible with this, but if you see your child struggling, give them a prompt and take it that they are now struggling to recall what comes next. We want them to experience mastery over the play task so suggest that this will be the end of the game. Aim for as lengthy a list as possible as this increases the challenge while also extending the duration of engagement. You might end up between you with: *'We went on a picnic and we brought sandwiches, hard-boiled eggs, crisps, chocolate, water, a blanket to sit on, a ball to play with, doughnuts, fruit, sun cream, our swimsuits.'* Saying 'we' instead of 'I' is a modification that allows you to work collaboratively and to emphasise that it is about doing something together. This one works with one child or many children. You can play this face to face, sitting around the dinner table or while in the car together.

Activities that embody rhythm and synchrony activate those sub-systems of the developing brain associated with emotional regulation. This is why they are so effective at repairing a ruptured connection in your parent–child relationship when the middle childhood brain is changing so much and you will be witness to some pretty impressive mood swings from your child. These types of activities will also help to keep play and playfulness an active part of your relationship at this tween stage.

Think about clapping games: **A sailor went to sea**; **Miss Mary Mack**; **the cup game** (this can be played in pairs or in as small or large a group as you choose); **Sevens** (this is a game of seven sets of sequences that run one after the other, each set becoming a little more challenging that the one that came before it); **Tic-tac-toe** (a sequence of hand clapping with lots of touching each other's hands, so this is an especially nice one); **Concentration** (where you take turns picking a topic while clapping each participant who must name things within that topic without repeating what anyone else has said); **Say, say oh playmate** (this one has a song – you might know it as Cee Cee My Playmate but that version's lyrics aren't so innocent so try the modified version here).

If some of these sound familiar from your own time on the playground in school, you can see how nice it is to be able to share with your child a game that you played yourself. However, if they do not sound familiar or you have forgotten how they are played, fear not, they are all up on my YouTube channel (you can find details at the end of the book) with tutorials breaking down how to play them.

With all of these rhythm and synchrony activities you can use a more complex clapping pattern based on your child's – and your own – ability to sustain the rhythm for a period of time. Equally, you can modify to make the clapping pattern very basic so it is easier to sustain for longer periods of time. But don't worry if you get all tangled up doing this, as you will find your own rhythm and the collapse and collision of hands can be fun too.

When your child reaches 11 years old, the physical changes are in full swing for both boys and girls. This is a good time to increase nurture-based play (communicating – by doing rather than saying – that the child is deserving of good care and that you are there to take care of them) as a means of playfully approaching the subject of personal hygiene and self-care, which should now be handled by your child with increased privacy, though likely still requiring your active encouragement.

---

15 minutes of nurture play ideas

Activities such as **mini manicure/pedicure** – get a basin of warm soapy and scented water and soak the hands/feet in there. Don't be afraid to be playful with this and do a hand-stack in the water, scoop bubbles up and pass them from your hand to your child's and back again, or measure their foot up against your hand to see how big their foot is compared to your hand – these are also nice ways of increasing the touch as well as playfulness. Have a soft towel to hand and gently dry the hands/feet applying a gentle yet firm pressure and then, using some nice lotion or oil, rub into the hands/feet applying the same gentle yet firm pressure as you squeeze and rub the hands and fingers or feet and toes. Then apply some nail polish (clear if schools have a no colour polish rule) and hold the hands/feet in your own hands as you lightly blow on them to dry the polish. This is a really lovely nurturing and regulating activity. The type of pressure you use here is important. This is called **proprioceptive touch**, which is essential when it comes to physical and emotional regulation. Proprioception is the sense that gets stimulated through receptors in our skin that then communicates to our bodies and brains where we are in a given space, both in relation to others and to the world around us. It helps to centre and ground us. This deep pressure touch (it should be deep enough to really feel it but never so deep that it hurts) instils a sense of 'felt safety' and reassures the child that they are deserving of good and kind care.

Other activities that support this nurture area through proprioceptive touch include **Weather report,** whereby you have your child turn their back to you and either on their bare skin or through their T-shirt if it is more comfortable for them, you apply touch in the style of weather. For example, *it's raining* (you drum lightly around their back with your fingertips); *there's thunder rolling in* (using the edge of your two hands you make chopping movements across their back); *it's cloudy* (using both hands make grabbing type movement around their back); *a light breeze becomes very windy* (blow lightly then harder on their back/back of neck while your hands swish over and back across their backs; *it's sunny* (using the palm of one hand, make large circles on their back). You can do this as a **Pizza,** making a large circle with your finger and adding on a variety of toppings with your hands, changing the pressure of the touch each time and naming what you are adding. Give them some control over the activity by inviting the child to choose what weather or toppings they would like 'extra' of at the end.

This type of play might seem a little 'childish' for this age group, but I have never had a child (or even teenager) object to this type of activity when I am working with a family. Sometimes, we think something is too silly or childish for our children when what we mean is it might feel silly for us to do it with an older child. So try it and go with the reaction of *your* child in the moment and just because they reject it once doesn't mean they wouldn't willingly accept it from you another day.

Developmentally this is a good time to invest in strengthening the trust in your parent–child relationship. It will stand you in good stead when the even more testing teenage phase arrives. Do this by assigning more opportunity for independence, which I have mentioned above and will discuss further in Chapter 6. But do it playfully as well, using the following game to also achieve a **15-minute play experience** between you and your child. Scatter obstacles around the room (cushions/toys/beanbag) and blindfold them, saying they should move according to your voice and direction. They have to carefully attune to you and what you are advising them and trust that you will get them across the space safely. This is a nice activity to reinforce this message.

It is also around this age that they start to show increased engagement in risk-taking behaviour. Risk is a key developmental milestone in adolescence, and far from dissuading them from taking risks, you want to start spotlighting opportunities for healthy risk-taking behaviour (Chapter 1 talks more about risk). Increased independence and privacy bring with it triumph and failure, both of which are important learning curves. Morality, good and bad, right and wrong, success and failure are all important themes around now, and developing a healthy relationship to risk is vital.

As their relationship with risk is further explored, you might find that while they still see and accept you as a figure of authority, they are more inclined to directly challenge you on many things. They may well seem defiant or oppositional here, and although it can be extremely frustrating and provocative for parents, this is actually more evidence of the risk-taking behaviour that begins to emerge at this stage of development. Deal with this by offering increased opportunity for the young person to make decisions, within your parental boundaries. Don't criticise a choice even when you feel it is the wrong one (unless it could be harmful or detrimental of course) but moreover allow the mistake to happen so the learning and self-correction of behaviour can emerge.

Eleven-year-olds realise that there are multiple ways to consider a given situation and they are not afraid to highlight this point to you! This means they will become more argumentative in asserting their own increased authority. They will begin to use phrases and make references that are outside your family's and perhaps your beliefs, showing that they are increasingly influenced by their peers and the media they are exposed to. This is a good time to start practising the vital adolescent parenting skill of *picking your battles*.

Play interests change beyond the imaginative world and they will invest more time in particular hobbies that they feel passionate about. Let them choose something that they really like and give it energy and focus, even if you are despairing that they are walking away from piano and instead devoting themselves solely to tag rugby or sea scouts. What matters most is that they maintain a hobby for as long as you can keep them engaged in it. It is also really important that they get to express their own desire in this regard. You will also see that 'play' for your tween is more about 'hanging out' and that this is deemed in and of itself an activity, though you may not see much action happening. This will be sleepovers or going to shopping centres with friends, or group outings with peers to the cinema.

Because of this, avoid over-scheduling your child and support their desire and curiosity by agreeing to fewer activities and more unstructured down time with friends. Have their friends over, let them spend time in your kitchen making pizzas and then taking those pizzas into a room in your house to eat and watch movies and chat, with the door closed. They can be with you and apart from you all at once, and this is a good practice to set up now as it will be a way of ensuring that they bring friends into your home knowing they can have privacy while you know they are close by.

While your 11-year-old is starting to show much more interest in themselves and their own lives and friends, they are not yet (generally) avoidant of family time so use this (narrowing) window to maintain your 15 minutes of play using some of the following activities.

Spider's web: This is a lovely group/family activity to play. Everyone sits in a circle on the floor. Take a ball of wool/yarn/roll of crepe paper and start with you. Say, 'I would like to thank Kerrie for emptying the dishwasher today without being asked to do it. It really helped me,' and wrapping the wool around your finger, pass or lightly toss the ball to her. Kerrie then names another family member across from her and thanks them for doing something that helped her that day or week and wraps the wool around her finger and passes it across. Repeat this so that everyone has thanked and been thanked by each other. Now the last person passes back to you and you snip the end of the wool and wrap that loose end around another finger. Invite everyone to slowly lift the wool to show the web of gratitude you have weaved together. Extend this game by placing a balloon in the middle and, using the web, the group will toss and catch the balloon when you say 'toss' and 'catch'. When done, gently lay the web on the ground and help each other out of it. This is your family web of shared gratitude and appreciation but also shows your interconnectivity and dependence on each other as a unit – *this is a lovely one to play with a blended family to help bring everyone together!*

Add in some nurture: A nice added step here is to take the wool from your web and turn it into a pom-pom – the ones you make with two matching circles of card with the centres cut out and you wrap the wool around to use it all up then carefully cut between the two circles and tie a piece of wool around the centre before sliding the card off (this is definitely easier to grasp if you search online for a quick video tutorial on it). Now save the pom-pom or attach a wool loop so that you can hang it somewhere. This is a great way to keep your web of connection alive, or you can even use this to play some of the nurture-based cotton-ball touch games listed in the first book (cotton-ball touch, cotton-ball face massage, cotton-ball/feather guessing, cotton-ball blow) but use your family pom-pom instead.

Pass the pulse around the group one way and then the other and then two pulses at once. The aim is to stay still, keep the eyes shut and, holding each other's hands, work to tune into each other and get that pulse/squeeze around the group. Give this a few attempts. It is important to laugh at the failures (when you get one or many more pulses back) rather than correct them. This is about coming together, holding hands and working as a connected group to achieve a task – it should be fun!

Pass a message (a – by touch, and b – by whisper): There are two ways to do this and I suggest doing both to really maximise your 15-minute potential here. Start with the touch approach. Stand or sit in a circle and everyone turns to their right so they are facing someone's back. Everyone just looks straight ahead (close the eyes if this helps). You start by tracing a simple message (a letter, number, shape) on the back in front of you. That person must pass on how they received the message and then you get it back at the end. It is great fun to see how much it has or hasn't changed. Again, don't worry about accuracy but more about fun, laughter and participation here. Now repeat the experience by whispering something into the ear on one side of you and have that person pass along the whisper until you get it back. Again, it's great fun to see what happened to the message along the way. **Tip:** Remember to send each message both ways around the group. In other words, if you start sending it to the right, do a second round to the left. In small group/family play, it is really nice that everyone gets to give to and receive from each other.

GOOD ENOUGH IS GOOD ENOUGH

Playing together as a family is vital to support healthy relationships at home. Realistically, it can be hard to secure 15 minutes with each of your children individually every day, so some days 15 minutes of play as a family is as good as it gets, and that is okay. Further, when it comes to middle childhood, when 'play' is starting to feel *too babyish* to your tween and as you prepare to allow them to pull away from you in their adolescence, this kind of small group/family play is less intense and more structured, which can make it easier for your tween to engage. This approach can be very supportive of the sibling relationship(s) too, which this middle-childhood phase can put under significant stress when your child might be irritated by their younger siblings and not yet cool enough for the older ones. In this increasingly digital age, we can tell the difference between a real moment of meeting (connection) between us and our children and one that feels flatter, when you are trying to reach out and they are absorbed in their devices. It is the same from the child's perspective – they know when we are authentically available and open to connecting with them and when we are just simply 'trying' because we should or feel we should. Family play offers the opportunity for *shared joy* and connection with each other that may be hard to secure otherwise during your day.

Your child's friendships are beginning to change and evolve in this middle-childhood phase as well, and groups start to play a more dominant role in their world. This will be explored further in Chapter 2 but engaging in family group play together so that group dynamics and the child's role within a group can be experienced also supports this phase.

A SECOND BITE AT THE DEVELOPMENT APPLE

At 12 years old, physical changes are at their peak for both boys and girls, with physical and emotional puberty in full swing. They are entering a phase of rediscovering and redefining who they are both for themselves and in relationships with those around them.

You will see clear evidence of rebelliousness and independence seeking, but I want to reframe that as a time for developing leadership skills. The child will have a good sense of community and that others are not as well off as they might be (socially, financially or otherwise) and it would be nice family practice to select a shortlist of charities and allow your tween to select one that your family will work for or support over the year. When rebelliousness, independence seeking and leadership drives converge, it is more important than ever before that you hold gentle yet firm boundaries in place. Be clear about your expectations and what any consequences for family rule-breaking will be. Expect and anticipate them testing you on this too.

Preferred play is increasingly about screen time and hanging out with friends. Keeping a playful connection alive is really important here but traditional play may be dismissed as childish. This is when I suggest you reach for challenge-based play to keep your 15-minute play active.

A CHALLENGING TIME CALLS FOR CHALLENGING PLAY

Challenge-based play is play that supports your child's developing self-esteem and efficacy. It is play that shows your child all that they are capable of and that it is worth pushing themselves a little outside their comfort zone for the sense of achievement. It supports risk-taking as well. I advocate challenge play that is collaborative and well within your child's developmental capacity as we want them to experience mastery over the task. However, at this age you can afford to add a more competitive edge to this type of play so consider two teams within your family and there will be collaboration between the team members but competition between each team. Also consider ways that you can embed challenge within other types of activities you will be doing. Increasing the level of challenge within the play also serves to keep your child engaged and interested in the play itself.

Mirrors with challenge added: Stand opposite and facing your child (tall kneel if better for eye contact and your knees can take it) and invite them to (non-verbal, movement only) mirror exactly what you do. You can embed the challenge here by having your child stand/balance on two or three cushions while they maintain focus on being your mirror.

Tug-of-war: You can do this with two of you or, if more, in two teams. Take a long scarf or piece of material or stretch out a skipping rope. Each person holds one opposing end. At your say so you each pull the rope. Don't use ready, steady, go or 1, 2, 3 go but increase the connection and attunement by cueing them with a word: 'When I say your name (or something) we pull.' Depending on the age and physicality of your child (I have lost many many rounds of this without needing to consciously *let* them win) you can ensure that if you are 'winning' you pull them over and into your embrace and if they are winning, you seek to 'tumble' into them for a hug – or a high five if more comfortable for them.

Beanbag balance with challenge added: Take a (tossable) beanbag or two. Use beanie teddies (small ones if that's what you have) and place them on your child's head. Invite them to stand, if they aren't already, and remember that moving from kneeling or seated into a standing position with a beanbag balanced on your head is already an increased challenge. Now that they are standing you direct them around the space you are in: *Two steps forward... tiptoe to the right... do a deep squat then stand... turn around... walk backwards.* How much challenge you introduce will be dependent on your child's capacity as this is one you can grow as their capacity grows.

Twelve-year-olds are capable of greater degrees of logic and abstract thought, critical thinking and problem-solving but remember that the pre-frontal cortex part of the brain is still very immature so flashes of temper, emotional meltdowns, signs of erratic and inconsistent intolerance and irritation will also be evident. They will also show signs of pronounced emphasis on justice and fairness (very much as they see it) and will demand that you justify and explain your parental decisions as they relate to them. Again, pick your battles, and this is a time that once you have explained your choice (usually around why they cannot do something or go somewhere that 'all their friends' can go) you say, 'I have told you why. You now know the reason.' And finally, 'because I said so' is now an acceptable answer.

They will now begin to experiment with tastes and lifestyle choices quite apart from your own. This is when your 12-year-old announces that they are now vegan and you are immoral for eating meat. They may decide that they want to abandon your religious/spiritual practices if you have them or take some up if you do not. Encourage curiosity but ensure that it is active and that they are a part of the choice. What I mean is that you are not googling all the vegan recipes but encouraging them to join you in the process to explore and learn together. You do not support their political cause or new religious choice but will help them research and find out more about it, even attending a local group a few times with them and reflecting on what was said there afterwards.

Try to look on middle childhood as an opportunity to fine-tune your child's development in preparation for adolescence. Focus on opportunities for increased independence, healthy risk-taking, trying-failing-trying again-learning, chances to self-correct their behaviour. Start (gradually) handing over responsibility for personal hygiene and begin to include your tween in conversations about world events and life stuff; basically, ask them what they think and feel about things going on around them.

Play is essential here. It underpins and supports the physical, emotional, social and neurological changes that are going on and allows you to maintain and indeed sustain a playful parent–child connection while you start to redefine the boundaries of your relationship in line with their development.

Essentially, middle childhood is a time of transition, and emotional (and physical) maturity levels will vary greatly, so trust your parental instinct as to what feels right for you and your child here – as always, YOU are the expert on your child, but if in doubt, *reach out* and seek consultation and support from your GP, teachers, child psychotherapist/psychologist as appropriate.

CHAPTER 1

Risk

Risk is a major milestone in adolescent development (more on that in book three) but the groundwork for the relationship to risk begins in early childhood and we must grow it in line with our children's growth. Take, for example, when your baby starts to crawl – or stand and wobble – you may have been blessed with a climber, a child who sees every standing piece of furniture and window sill in your house as an invitation.

Simply put, risk-taking behaviour is making a choice or taking an action when the outcome of that choice or action is unknown and cannot be fully predicted. It involves anything with an inherent chance of success or failure from the outset, which you decide to do anyway. After the early years, risk-taking can evolve into making new friends, joining a sports team, learning to cycle a bike or use roller skates. Risk-taking can also play out more negatively in behaviours such as stealing, lying, cheating. Later, in early to mid-adolescence, this can involve drinking alcohol, experimenting with drugs and sex, excessive dieting or self-harming behaviours.

In parenting, at all ages but especially this middle-childhood age, you will want to encourage healthy risk-taking behaviour to prepare for the draw of the negative risk-taking behaviour later on.

Risk-taking behaviour is the convergence of two motivational systems. One system is the one that renders a person sensitive to punishment while the other renders a person sensitive to reward.

The three stages of developmental play are what ultimately enable our children to regulate and balance the two systems. Let us look now at those stages of play.

Stage one is that stage of messy, tactile sensory play including sand water, bubbles, Play-Doh and music. This play that sees your child more fascinated with the box the toy came in than the box itself because boxes are all about containment and discovering what is on the inside versus outside. This stage of play is about discovering where 'I' end and the world and others outside me begin.

Stage two is where we see our children deepen their understanding of the world outside them by beginning to take in and consider the perspectives of others. They play with little dolls (small-world type play) and have them talk to and interact with each other. Being able to consider the perspectives of others is essential to developing empathy, critical thinking, reciprocity and general civility.

Stage three play is role play but be careful to see this as dramatic play rather than dressing-up play. This type of play is where the play decides what the prop is – for example, a scarf is never just a scarf: it is a magic carpet, a picnic blanket, a bandage, a blanket for a baby or a cape for a superhero – rather than the prop deciding what the play is, such as wearing a princess dress that makes me that princess and nothing else. In stage three play, our children push boundaries and test out what it would be like if they were in other roles in their lives, be that playing at being a parent or a doctor, a teacher, a musician or a builder.

These stages will take them up to seven years old to work their way through and it is only by working through each of these stages that our children are able to develop the all-important capacity to self-regulate their own emotional arousal. This is where this capacity is really tested. If your child is still grappling with emotional self-regulation, you will want to actively guide them for a while here. If however you feel your child is capable then allow them to engage in healthy levels of risk and reinforce the draw to healthy risk and those rewards being more deserving of their energy.

PARENTAL RISK SELF-AUDIT

First, take some time to stop and reflect on your own relationship with risk. Are you more driven and motivated by reward or punishment? (Note that this is not in any way intended to be a psychological measure or assessment tool, it is purely for personal and self-reflective use.)

1. Do you feel strongly motivated by money?
2. Is it difficult for you to send a meal back or make a complaint in a restaurant?
3. If you think that something is against the rules, would it stop you doing it?
4. Does alcohol feature strongly in your social life?
5. Has a hangover ever prevented you from taking your child to their weekend activities?
6. Does how others might think/feel about you influence your actions?
7. Are you anxious or fearful in new situations? Would this cause you to withdraw from an activity/event?
8. Do you often do things to elicit praise from others, even if it is something you didn't want to do?
9. If something carries an equal measure of pleasure and potential harm, would you do it?
10. How would those who know you best describe you in terms of risk – a risk taker or a risk avoider?
11. When you were a child did you enjoy team sports? Meeting new people?

12. Do you often suggest new things to do or new ways of doing something?
13. Can you easily list three positive risk-taking behaviours and three negative risk-taking behaviours?
14. What kind of risks did you take when you were a teenager? Were you the instigator of these behaviours or a follower when someone else suggested them?
15. Have you ever shoplifted? How did it feel before/during/afterwards?
16. Have you ever been arrested? How did it feel for you? What happened afterwards?
17. Do you find it easy to speak in public?
18. Is it easy for you to ask for a rise at work?
19. How do you feel when you see children fall and hurt themselves? What do you do/say?
20. How do you feel/behave when attending your child's sports/activities?

Understanding your own relationship to risk-taking behaviour is really helpful when it comes to parenting your child through this phase. If you are risk avoidant you may pass this hesitation and avoidance down to your children or if you are a big risk-taker without consideration of consequences you are, again, modelling this as a template for your children. We want children to take risks, we want them to take chances and try new things in unfamiliar situations and environments. We want our children to try something new, even though they cannot predict the outcome ahead of time and even though they might fail. We want them to participate in team activities and sports where there is an in-built, inherent chance of winning and losing. We want them to take risks that are, at least mostly, positive risks rather than harmful negative ones.

For this to happen, parents must lead by positive example. We have to embrace risk, embrace failing as much as succeeding and speak about what failing teaches us. Being avoidant of risk is not the positive alternative to taking risks. Being avoidant shows a fear that will make the risk-taking phase of adolescent development very difficult. If you have a child who is fearful and thus avoidant of risk, you must gently yet firmly find opportunity to practise small risk-taking behaviour and gradually build it up with and for them. If you have a reward-driven, impulsive risk-taker who shows little to no regard for outcomes or consequences, you will equally want to step in and modify their relationship to risk. You can do this by ensuring plenty of opportunity for safer, lower-level risk-taking and encourage them to hit their internal *pause* button before they act. Healthy risk is about balance. Healthy risk is enough fear to cause me to pause and consider the consequences but enough of a reward drive for me to see that the risk is worth engaging with because of what *might* happen and what I will learn regardless.

Protecting our children is one of our most basic instincts as a parent. But if we constantly jump in to rescue them, to do everything for them, how will they ever learn to manage challenges that come their way in life as they grow and develop? How will they learn to withstand peer pressure and stand their ground when faced with a decision as to whether they should join in with the group or walk away and go home?

Picture this scene and while you do, pay attention to what gets stirred up inside you as I describe it to you. I want you to visualise yourself doing exactly as I write now, even if this isn't your natural instinct.

You are standing in the child-friendly end of the swimming pool beckoning your child to come and join you. Your child approaches the edge of the pool and freezes. They refuse to come any further. They call out, 'I can't', 'I'm scared', 'Lift me in', or 'Come get me'. You stay exactly where you are. You do not move. You smile and wave them in towards you. They shake their heads. You say, 'Come on in, you can do this, just sit down at the edge and slide yourself in. I'm right here.' They shake their head and the lip starts to tremble as their eyes fill with tears. 'PLEASE come get me.' You stay exactly where you are and smile, waving them in and repeat, 'Come on in, you can do this, just sit down at the edge and slide yourself in. I'm right here.' Two minutes pass – that is 120 whole seconds. All you do is stay and smile in that time, regardless of what your child is saying now. Then, your child sits at the edge of the pool, slides in and walks over to where you are still standing. 'I DID IT!' they beam.

How are you feeling? At what point in this scenario did you feel yourself becoming anxious or irritated? What would you have done differently and why? What might the benefit be of playing it out as above?

In order for a child to overcome their fears we, their parents and important caregivers, must be patient and use our very presence and subtle encouragement to reassure them. This way they know and feel they are not alone but must dig deep within themselves for a solution. Children need daily opportunities to practise dealing with (reasonable and developmentally matched) risks because this is what helps them to grow and develop into capable young people who are well positioned to cope with the risks of adolescence. We are also subtly but consistently empowering them to attune to and trust their instincts and capabilities, which helps build self-confidence and efficacy.

How do you know if the risk is reasonable and developmentally matched to your child? Ask yourself (and answer), *What is the worst that could happen here? What is the benefit and potential learning from this risk situation?*

THE BENEFITS OF RISK-TAKING BEHAVIOUR

There are so many benefits to encouraging and creating opportunities for your children to engage in risk-taking behaviour, not least of which, as already mentioned, is to do with laying some vital groundwork for the neurological rewiring that is beginning now in middle childhood but will significantly increase come the onset of adolescence. But there are other pro-social benefits in this stage of development that are worth holding in mind. These include, but are not limited to:

- **Encouraging critical thinking and reflective practice:** In considering a risky behaviour, your child must take pause and ask themselves what is likely to happen if they do this. If it is something like climbing a tree, the pause will be brief and the process one of quick decision-making, which is itself an important life skill to learn because it requires that the child attunes to and acts on their own instincts. Being able to take risks and pause to reflect on the outcome afterwards is great practice for developing their instincts and strategic thinking as they grow up and start to consider risks with bigger stakes.

- **Supporting physical development:** The human brain is a fascinating organ and is actually hardwired to motivate a person to take the requisite actions necessary for whole-brain development. In this regard, children are motivated instinctually to take risks as a way of fine-tuning and enhancing their fine and gross motor skill development, their coordination skills and physical flexibility. In taking risks, children learn to fall, get up and learn how to fall safely or modify the risk to avert a fall; in this way, personal safety awareness can grow too. Reasonable and appropriate risk-taking provides a sensory stimulus that allows young bodies and brains to thrive and surge forward developmentally.

- **Strengthening social skills development:** As we know, in adulthood sometimes the big risk to take is to be able to find and use your voice in a crowd. Now is a great time to start taking social risks. This can be supported by encouraging participation in an extracurricular activity outside school and in typical peer groups where your child will have to mix with new children. You can encourage them to initiate play with children they meet in playgrounds and to simply place their own order to the serving staff when in a café or restaurant, or approach the cash register to pay for their own items in a shop. At home, ensure you are encouraging them to state their opinion on something and react to it so that they get to hear how others may think the same or differently from them.

- **Cultivating confidence and self-efficacy:** It is an essential element of psychological resilience to experience the euphoria of success, the disappointment of failure and the value of perseverance in bridging the two. Reasonable risk-taking allows a child of this age to integrate fully that they are able to overcome obstacles and work out solutions to their own problems and challenges.

- **Defending against the unhealthy risks ahead:** Learning to engage with and even embrace reasonable and healthy risks now in middle childhood helps to ensure that your child is better equipped to say no to unhealthy risks that will present themselves later on in adolescence. Developing a healthy understanding of risk in this experiential way of 'doing' helps them to integrate a stronger instinctual sense of what is right for them and empowers them to say no when faced with something negatively risky.

It is very important that your child develops a sense of agency, and investing in reasonable risk-taking in early – and increasingly in middle – childhood is a great way to kick-start this. Having 'agency' means that a child can learn to act independently and take responsibility for their own actions while making their own free choices. It allows children to develop self-esteem, a stronger sense of self (understanding who they are in the world and in relation to the people around them) and emotional well-being. Being able to make choices and decisions for themselves ensures they feel that they can influence events that affect them and that they can have an effect on the world they live in. It ensures that children view themselves as competent and contributing members of society. As it is the job of parenting to raise children to grow into independent adults, it is certainly worth taking a risk on risk.

Throughout this chapter, I have referred to 'risk' in terms of 'reasonable risk'. What I mean by this is that in order for risk-taking to be developmentally effective, it must first of all be developmentally matched. When it comes to play that supports risk-taking, I focus on challenge-based activities *but* these activities are mostly challenge that is collaborative rather than competitive. Where it is competitive it tends to involve play between two teams so that you have competition between the teams but collaboration within each team. I also advise that you start by setting challenge-based play tasks that are well within your child's developmental reach and gradually increase the challenge bit by bit. Remember, we want to use this type of play to support and build confidence and self-esteem, to convey that all-important sense of *wow, look at all you can do* and *it is exciting to put yourself out there and take a chance on something*.

If you are a risk-averse or very competitive parent this is something you have to gently, yet firmly, challenge in yourself. Always remember that our children take their social and emotional cues from us, their parents and key caregivers, so we must lead by positive example. If you are risk averse, pause to reflect on why this might be. Is it a part of your own story of growing up and being parented? What did risk mean to you? There are ways of starting with small and playful risk (see below) that might enable you to gradually increase this capacity in yourself. If you have a partner to co-parent or a friend/family member who can provide hands-on help, let them lead some of this risk-taking play while you observe until it feels comfortable to go there yourself. For those competitive parents – you know who you are – you will want to focus on the collaborative play, with all your energy and verbal reinforcements going on effort over outcome. No goals or keeping score for you, not yet anyway. Again, lean on a less competitive co-parent/friend/family member who can model calmer more collaborative play. Here are some suggestions below.

SMALL AND PLAYFUL RISK – GAME IDEAS

Take 15 minutes

Cushion balance/jump: Place one cushion on the floor and have your child stand on it and centre themselves (easy). Praise the effort: 'Great idea to stand in the middle of the cushion for balance.' Have them jump off (either into your arms to build in a bit of nurture or into a beanbag if they are bigger or more high energy – mind yourself too). Now place a second cushion on top of the first one and repeat. Change your praise a little each time, still emphasising the effort over the outcome. Build up by one cushion each time until you see that they start to struggle, then you move in and say, 'This time I want you to balance on the cushions while holding my shoulder with one arm.' You know you are stabilising them but the way you say it makes it a logical part of the activity so that the sense of achievement is sustained.

A more downwards regulating activity to play is **cotton-ball pick up**, which is good when you have a more introverted child or you want to bring your higher energy child down a bit. Take your child's socks off and place a cotton ball on the floor in front of them. Tell them they have to pick it up with their toes and raise their foot up and back down, or place the ball into your cupped hand. Once they have achieved this with one cotton ball, place two cottons balls together and repeat. Continue by adding a new cotton ball each time until you see them start to struggle (usually five is the maximum for this one). If they fail, praise the effort and take responsibility by saying, 'I made that too difficult. Let's repeat it with up to four cotton balls with your other foot.' Again, focus on *praising effort over outcome* with phrases such as, 'Ooh I can see you're taking your time to make sure you grab and hold them all – that's a great idea.'

A different spin on this one is to take a handful of cotton balls and scatter them around the room/floor space. You sit in one spot and stay there and ask your child(ren) to hop around on one foot and pick up one cotton ball at a time with their other foot and hop/bring it all the way over to you. They then repeat this until all the cotton balls have been retrieved, one at a time. To bring some mild competition into this one for the slightly older end of this age group (who enjoy the competitive edge more), colour your cotton balls (with a felt-tip marker) and see who can return theirs the quickest. If you happen to have a small group of four or more children (either your own or when there is a party or play date), separate them into teams and see which team can achieve the task the fastest – remember to increase the volume of cotton balls for larger groups.

Another game I like to use in this area of risk involves both *risk* and *trust* and is my version of **blindman's buff**. I show the child around the space. While they are looking I show them how I am adding some (safe) obstacles to the floor such as cushions or soft toys. Next I say I would like to cover their eyes so that they can't see and I will use my voice to direct them from one side of the room to me. A degree of trust must exist before you do this game. Your child must trust that you will guide and direct them safely around the room.

Some **family board games** that have inherent risk built in (anything with a chance of winning or losing is risky) can also be good. I especially like games where strategy is of no use and it is pure risk with roll of a dice, such as **Snakes and Ladders**. I also think the children's versions of **charades** (you can make this with random things written on scraps of paper placed in a bowl rather than buying a packaged game) or **Cranium** (this requires a mix of efforts as teams work in creative, data/ knowledge, word play and performance-style challenges) contain the risk of performing, having to convey meaning in a non-verbal way, work collaboratively with others and challenges children to come up with creative solutions to these risks. I also think the game **Guess Who** is a good one as it requires participants to use descriptive questions to work out the solution. **Buckaroo!** is a good one for fine motor skills and also tests a low frustration threshold.

CHAPTER 2

Middle Childhood and Friendship

I will start this chapter by emphasising that, with rare exception, you should stay out of your children's friendships. Friendship is a developmental curve in and of itself and it evolves significantly throughout childhood. They will be in sync and out of sync and back in sync (or perhaps not) and this will repeat. It is not, again with very rare exception, helpful for your child if you insert yourself into their friendships, negotiate boundaries on their behalf or rescue them from rows they have with friends. This also means that you may have to bite your tongue, so to speak, if you see your child making a friendship choice you would not make for them. These are not *your* friends to choose, these are not your mistakes to make, and if you don't allow your child to make them they cannot learn how to negotiate their own relationship boundaries.

The rare exceptions I am referring to here are, of course, where you know your child to be involved in bullying (either as victim or perpetrator). Then you should step in and act on what you know by bringing it to the attention of the school or activity coordinator or other parents. Bear in mind that bullying is repeated, targeted behaviour by one person against another or by a group against a person or by one person who incites others to isolate another. Children will be mean and rude to each other, and while that is deeply unpleasant, it is not the same as bullying. This was discussed in more detail in book one.

Friendship is really important in developing self-esteem and competency as a child and this is certainly needed in this middle-childhood phase. You will also observe a tendency towards same-gender friendships between ages eight and 12 years because friendships in middle childhood are largely based on similarities they feel they share with others. You might observe an increasing or even brand-new emergence of intolerance towards those your child does not feel they have much in common with, those who are dissimilar to them. This is also why I am flagging the subtle yet distinct differences between bullying and rudeness/meanness because rude and mean tend to naturally increase during this phase of development. This prejudicial rigidity tends to be a passing phase as your child is deepening their understanding of who they are and who they like to be around, so focus on gently challenging it but do not panic that your child is becoming sociopathic.

Research[1] has shown that it is friendship reciprocity that especially enhances self-esteem and positive attitude and outlook towards others. This means that it is more helpful to your child's development if their feelings towards and desire for someone to be their friend/best friend are reciprocated by the other child(ren).

This is a good time to pause and reflect on your own friendships in your childhood and even now.

- How important are friends to you?
- Do you meet up with friends on a regular basis?
- Are your friends connected to specific areas of your life, i.e. via the school your children attend/work/couples you know with your partner/neighbours?
- Do you have a 'go-to' person you know you can call on when you need to?
- Do you have someone you immediately want to share good/bad news with?
- How long is your oldest friendship?

- Do you remember your first real friend? How old were you? Can you recall the story of how you met and what you liked about this person? How did it make you feel then and how does it make you feel now to recall this? Do you still know this person? Have your feelings changed about them? Are you still active in each other's lives? What is the story about this development?
- Did you struggle with friendship as a child or in school?
- Do you hold particular views about nice kids and mean kids? Bring one such child to mind and ask yourself, *Who is this child for me? Who do they remind me of in my life?* and pause to consider if you might be projecting unresolved feelings for someone else onto them.
- Do you have views on the type of child you want your own child to be friends with? How do you manage this?

Now imagine that your child asks to bring a new school friend home to play. You agree. When the child arrives they are not who you want your child playing with (you decide why this might be or what behaviour or other attribute might evoke this feeling for you). Now reflect on how you feel about this and what you believe you would do or say, if anything, about this to effect a change?

FRIENDS – HOW TO MAKE THEM AND HOW TO KEEP THEM

Deepening your understanding of and awareness of your own relationship to friendships and the roles friends play in your life will help you to see if you are maybe seeking to fix something about yourself through your child's friendships. Friendship is really important to us as parents, as people. We need to have our own friends and ideally one friend who is not connected to us through the school gate or work but just somebody who is in our life because we click and connect with each other as people (not as parents or as colleagues, though of course meaningful friendships can be forged in these contexts too). It is important for us to take a step back and allow our children to develop this value for friendships in their life themselves and to explore all kinds of friends to find out who they most like to be around, who brings out the best in them and who makes them feel as if someone 'gets' them. We must let them get hurt, disappointed and let down, and support them as they cry and mourn that loss, helping them to reflect so that they can integrate the learning and have it guide them as they make more friends.

Equally, we should allow them to explore what it is like to befriend someone who might (seemingly) be entirely different from who they are and rather than assess (or even assert) that this child isn't a suitable friend, sit after the play date and wonder with them about what they like best about spending time together. We should step back and observe quietly but knowingly as our children reach out to the so-called cooler kids (maybe yours *is* the cool kid). This will allow them to work through their natural desire to fit in or be accepted by peers and perhaps even to be looked up to by others without you putting meaning onto this behaviour for them. This social experimentation with peers and groups is important because it is a key part of their middle-childhood journey to deepen their own understanding of who they are and who others around them are. Exploring, testing, defying, redefining limits allows them to grow into adolescents who, at least, know that limits exist.

By middle childhood, your child is showing that they are able to consider multiple perspectives at once (you might recall how the capacity to do so is developed in stage two of developmental play, at approximately four years old). However, they will still struggle to hold two conflicting perspectives in mind at the same time. They will be aware of their own thoughts and feelings and of their friends' thoughts and feelings but they will not hold that dual awareness at the same time. This means it will be very difficult for them to figuratively step back and identify patterns in their friendships (good or bad) and they need help with this. The best way for you to do this is not to jump in and tell them how it is but rather hold back and gently wonder with them about certain patterns and themes you have observed: 'David was late today and you were waiting for him. I wonder how that made you feel? I wonder if you often feel like that?' If your child dismisses this and says everything was fine and they didn't mind, leave that alone. They will think about it themselves and a new awareness will be created so that they can draw their own conclusions. Maybe the answer is not what you think; maybe your child is fine with David being late because they know that David has a sibling with special needs who needs a lot of his parents' time and he often has to wait for them to be ready to take him somewhere. But by introducing a reflective question, you are modelling that they can reflect on how things and experiences make them feel.

Children of this age tend to have a pronounced sense of justice and fairness too. They firmly believe that if they do something nice for someone, that person ought to reciprocate directly and do something equally nice back. When that doesn't happen they can feel very let down by the friendship and perhaps even seek to terminate it and reject that child. Again, this is not the time to tell them not to be so harsh but rather to use your *wondering* reflective voice to empathise with how they are feeling and wonder why people don't always do something nice back straight away, seeking to normalise this kind of behaviour pattern. They may not 'get it' immediately and may persist in dropping the friend but with gentle persistence from you in encouraging the development of their own capacity for reflective functioning (that capacity to recall things from a position of fresh thinking and new perspective) they will work it out themselves.

Children in middle childhood can be sticklers for the rules and this can result in high levels of judgement of themselves and others. They can be very tough on themselves while holding others to their own (often impossibly) high standards. They will assert with certainty that the new outfit you just bought them will render them a social pariah and they cannot possibly wear it; if you insist you are 'RUINING MY LIFE'. You think of it as dramatic hysterics but this is very real for them; they truly believe that they will be rejected by their peers if they wear something they deem embarrassing, something that would make them stand out, because at this age, fitting in, blending in, is of the utmost importance. It is a good time to afford them some more choices around their clothing, hairstyles and so on. This should still be within your boundaries. You set a price limit to clothing choices (because you are paying) and tell them you have a final veto if you think the chosen item is not suitable (be that for a set occasion or in general).

Their peers are people 'like them' with lots of shared interests and outlooks, so it stands to reason that they tend to form things like closed groups or clubs. They may even give their 'club' a name and have a code of conduct or set of rules that group members must subscribe to. (*We wear pink on Wednesdays* comes to mind, a quote from *Mean Girls*, a 2004 American teen comedy written by Tina Fey). This is not something to worry about; this is quite normal and usually fleeting – the club name, rules and platform may change in quite a short space of time.

Children at this age will prioritise their peers. They invest heavily in them. They want to confide in and be confided in. They want to know and keep each other's secrets. They really care about each other's happiness and well-being and it can seem as if they are extensions of each other, being always together. This is a little more true and reflective of female friendships at this age than male ones but you will certainly observe some of these patterns in boys' friendships too, though perhaps not so intensely. Because the investment in friendship is so intense, a slight or a full-blown betrayal, even a perceived one, can deeply hurt them.

While the intensity increase is most pronounced in female friendships at this age, you will likely see an increase in boy's competitiveness too. This will suit some boys more than others. Using challenge-based play (such as the family games listed at the end of Chapter 1 with the collaborative approach but using teams such as parents against children or dividing into two teams each with a parent) can help build a child's capacity for this more competitive play so that they can better manage that dynamic.

When to recognise a friend has become a frenemy

Children's friendships tend to follow a general growth trajectory as they grow up and develop. This is normal, healthy and to be anticipated. There will most definitely be times when you will feel the urge to jump in and rescue them from a friendship you know is not in their interests. With rare exception, leave this alone so they can work out what type of friends complement them or not and who makes them feel good or bad about themselves, and allow them to reflect that while all people have motivations and perspectives, some will align with theirs and some won't. The rare exception is the toxic friendship that you can see is negatively affecting your own child's self-esteem and confidence and impacting on their quality of life, be that in school, at an activity or at home. In this instance, take steps to redirect your child towards other friends and speak with your school to see if changing class or even moving seat is an option and if the teacher can keep a watchful eye on the situation. Apart from this, parents really should stay out of their children's friendships.

I received a call from 11-year-old Kate's mother. She was highly stressed and what I would describe as quite fearful. She told me a story about her daughter's friendship with another child in her class at school – they had been friends for years, since they were six or seven years old, and while she would always have described the friend Charlotte as more dominant and assertive than Kate, she had no initial causes for concern about their friendship. She spoke further about how, as time went by, she had noticed very slow and gradual changes in Kate. She became increasingly withdrawn and nervous in her disposition. She seemed to need to run everything by Charlotte before she did it.

When I asked for an example of this, she told me about a plan she was making with Kate for her 11th birthday party. She was suggesting some options that she knew Kate would enjoy and said that Kate was rigid and immovable in not being able to make a final decision without talking to Charlotte first. Kate did this and her mum felt she chose the least 'Kate' of the three options but the most 'Charlotte'. She said this was when a lot of little niggles started to come together for her and she had spoken with Kate about her friendship with Charlotte and how it had now been a long time since she had mentioned other friends or brought anyone else from school home. She said that Kate froze, her eyes filled with tears and her lip trembled. She started to cry quietly and then a lot so that her whole body shook with the effort of it. Her mum was bracing herself for something awful. Kate spoke about how she was afraid of Charlotte, how Charlotte wouldn't allow her to make choices or decisions and told her what to wear each day and who she could talk to. Kate had justified this saying, 'I think it's just because I'm her very best friend but sometimes she just scares me.'

The story continued to unfold over the coming week as little by little Kate described the nature of her friendship with Charlotte, showing that Charlotte was more than dominant; she was controlling, and this friendship was toxic for Kate. Kate was adamant she didn't want her mum to discuss this with the school or with Charlotte's parents.

After our consultation her mum agreed with Kate not to discuss it with Charlotte's parents but that she would ask the teacher about moving Kate to a new class (this was an option in their school) and to keep an eye on things. Proactively, she encouraged Kate to choose two new activities to join up to, one in school to be around other children there with shared interests and one outside of it to broaden her social network outside the school community.

In this instance, I was just working with the mother as she wanted to make some changes herself and see how Kate was before deciding if she should be referred to me or not. We worked on therapeutic parenting responses to effect the change in Kate through her relationship with her mum. Mum described to me huge resistance from Charlotte in letting Kate go, but how sharing what was happening with her mum seemed to embolden Kate to make the separation. She said she never fell out with Charlotte but gradually made herself unavailable to her and invested in new friendships.

Her mum said she felt she had needed to actively insert herself into Kate's social world and friendships in a way she never had before and that this was hard for her. It was also important that she knew when to step back out, which she did, though she shared she was finding out what secondary school Charlotte would be going to before she confirmed one for Kate. This toxic friendship had a significant impact on Kate's self-esteem, confidence and quality of life. It left her with some anxiety-based behaviours that her mum had noticed, been curious and concerned about but couldn't understand until that birthday party incident. It was a number of months before the matter was truly resolved for Kate.

Toxic friendships can come from all kinds of motivations in the other child. In this instance, it seemed most likely that Kate's kind and compassionate nature made her an attractive friend for Charlotte, as she would be easy to dominate and control. Toxic friendships can go on for quite a long time before their impact is truly understood, as was the case here. It wasn't any one action but a pattern that was gradually chipping away at Kate's confidence and self-esteem and emotional well-being. This situation was escalating and would have continued to have an increasingly negative effect on Kate's emotional development and mental health had her mum not intervened. This is an instance when staying out of it is not the option, but thankfully such incidences are rare and, as with Kate's mum, knowing when to step back out – when Kate had returned to the path of more typical healthy development and friendships – is as important as knowing when to step in.

EMOTIONAL RESILIENCE

The reason I feel so strongly about parents stepping back and supporting our children in their evolving friendship choices and experiences is because it is so helpful in the children's development and refinement of emotional resilience at this stage of development. Being emotionally resilient will also help them to withstand and cope with rudeness and meanness, mild rejections and slights by friends, and the highs and lows of their day-to-day life and interactions with others. It is an essential life skill.

Being emotionally resilient is the ability to (emotionally) bounce back from disappointments and frustrations in life. It is an essential trait for all of us to develop but this starts in early childhood and really goes up a notch in its depth and sophistication during this middle childhood phase.

Emotional resilience develops in children when they know that they are in a safe, secure, predictable, calm, consistent and loving parent–child relationship. This is the foundation stone for resilience, which thrives on a strong emotional connection. It expands when a child is afforded opportunity for healthy risk-taking and independence. It flourishes when we resist the urge to fix all of our children's problems but sit with them and ask *wondering* questions that allow them to arrive at the solution for themselves. It multiplies when we reflect our children's emotional states (naming them) back to them: 'I understand that you're angry because this didn't go the way you wanted. I know you thought about it for a long time and wanted it to go well. I wonder if you're feeling sad and disappointed at the way it worked out too.' You are helping your child to deepen their own understanding of what is happening within themselves; you are reinforcing that our overt behaviours (shouting and hitting) are underpinned by an emotional state (anger/upset) and a physical state (having worked so hard at something, they are tired) while helping them to develop their emotional vocabulary so that they can better express themselves the next time. Emotionally resilient children have a strong emotional vocabulary.

You complete their emotional resilience framework by modelling good coping skills and embracing mistakes as opportunities to learn from. If you lead by positive example, this cements their resilience-building education. This means that you allow them to see (age appropriately of course) you make some types of mistakes and how you process and recover from them and emerge with new learning to try again. It is good for them to occasionally see you struggle with a problem, even a coordination issue such as how you will get two children to two different places at the same time, and work out a solution, especially one that involves you reaching out to someone for support and help. Letting them see (again in a developmentally appropriate manner) the highs and lows of your day teaches them a lot about how to handle what life throws and will throw at them. And if we accept that the job of parenting is to raise independent healthy functioning adults, then that work starts here with resilience building.

Emotionally resilient children can positively adapt to stress and adversity. This doesn't mean that they do not struggle with these events – they absolutely do – but their struggle does not derail them. They can emotionally self-regulate, which is to say that they can manage their feelings, even multiple feelings at the same time, and work within the rules (know what is expected of them and stick fairly well to that) and can largely control their own behaviour (or make quick and healthy repair following misbehaviour) and keep their impulsiveness in check. Now, let me be clear we are talking about 8–12-year-old children, not robots, so while emotionally resilient children have good, strong and consistent capacity to do all of this, they will of course wobble, make mistakes, have moments of falling apart and make some pretty poor choices at times that will make you stop and wonder if they 'get it' at all. The difference is that these incidents are more minor than those in less resilient children, and their recovery from these transgressions is much quicker and is generally fully experienced. What I mean by that is that the route to repair following rupture is fully experienced by them, they know that they have done wrong, can reflect on that and seek to repair it with the person they have wronged by taking responsibility and saying sorry rather than just insisting things are now magically okay and expecting you to meet them there.

Relational play – play between people rather than in isolation (like my 15-Minute Parenting model) – helps to build and support emotional resilience in children… and even adults, who will also benefit from daily play themselves. Children construct their identity through play – it allows them to explore and learn about who they are, what they like to do, what brings them joy and how to interact with the world and people around them. Play helps children to build their own network of peers and to nurture and grow their friendships because it is relational and intersubjective.

Consider the **Alphabet game** here as well because it encourages reciprocity and collaboration. Pick a topic such as musicians or book characters or movie characters (pick something your child will know about and be interested in) and then between you (a nice one to do sitting in the car side by side or out for a walk together or even with more people, because this is one that works in pairs as well as groups) take turns with each letter of the alphabet saying a musician whose name starts with that letter. The challenge is to see whether between you, can you make it from A–Z staying on topic. I like to build in a collaborative element to the challenge here by saying each player can avail of three passes whereby they can pass a letter they are stuck on to another team member who has an answer in order to keep the group moving and to prolong the engagement in the activity.

Physical play builds resilience through strengthening gross and fine motor skills.

Rough and tumble play that builds gross motor skills and coordination at this age can be facilitated by you developing a mini-assault/obstacle course in your garden using boxes of different heights to climb up and jump from, a net to crawl under, small blocks to balance on and walk across, a rope to pick up to skip with and things to jump over and run between. This can be as basic or complex as you need it to be.

Making flower or pasta jewellery builds the fine motor skills. Threading beads onto string together is a great way to do this. You can add in emotional benefits by colour coding your feelings (each colour is associated with a different feeling) and as you choose the colour bead you must share a story of a time you felt that feeling. Add in challenge by seeing if you can guess how many beads it would take to fill the piece of string and then put that amount onto the string to see how close you got to it.

For your 15-minute play as a family, you can make a knot with your hands that you must work together to untangle, without letting go of the hand you are holding. Start in a circle and everyone raises the left hand and reaches in to take the hand of someone else (not the person beside you). Now repeat with your right hand (not the same person). Now, try to untangle back into an open circle while holding on to the hands you have. This will work sometimes and not others; when it doesn't work, it is a good playful way to bring up and work out frustrations, and regardless of the result it is a great collaborative challenge to do as a family. You need five or more people for this to work.

This play supports confidence and competence, which is how this type of play supports the building of emotional resilience.

SYMBOLIC AND IMAGINATIVE PLAY

Symbolic or imaginative play also contributes greatly to the development of emotional resilience. Being able to pretend and imagine something helps children at this stage to differentiate between fantasy and reality, to understand and reflect on their own experiences, feelings and desires as well as those of the world and people around them. Pretending to be something and creating a world to enrich this fantasy is part of this play.

Build a fort indoors or outdoors: Allowing and encouraging children to make a den or fort out of furniture/sticks/a sheet and then retreating inside to play and imagine is lovely and fun. Indoors it can serve as a great rainy-day activity.

Cardboard boxes: Save them and allow your child to turn one into a television that they can sit behind and be a 'reporter' or 'actor' or 'TV star'. Perhaps they could make a large box into a car and sit in it 'driving' while you pull them around the room.

Assign a jigsaw puzzle: Work on a jigsaw as a family or between you or even set it for them alone. Alone play is important and should be a part of your child's play world, but not at a cost of your 15 minutes of parent–child play each day. You could choose a jigsaw that is a little (not a lot) outside your child's scope as a challenge and something to work towards. In this way, you could get a large complex jigsaw and simply leave it for each of you to add to as you pass it or are in the mood to on a given day.

Co-author a story: There are a few ways of doing this. I like to use story cubes, which are a set of dice with symbols on each side. You roll the dice and using the symbols that land face up, make up a story. I like to start with *Once upon a time* because it gives permission for anything to happen and invites your child to bring in the fantastical elements. Another way to do this is to take turns telling each other a line of a story. The parent can start with *Once upon a time there was a small house at the edge of a large forest* and then hand over for your child(ren) to add a line. Keep the story going for as long as it is fun and engaging, and when interest is waning, bring it to a close with *The end*. The important part here is not to judge what anyone else brings into the story, just accept it (even if this means that aliens have suddenly landed in the middle of a picnic when your last sentence had been about looking for a dog) and continue the story from the child's lead. You could also sit together and take time to write a book with structure (a cover, an index of chapters, illustrations, etc.).

It can be nice to start with one of the ways above and take them deeper into the narrative by suggesting you write it down and turn the story or stories into a book – only do this if writing a book is something that appeals to your child, and don't insist on writing it if it feels too school-like for your child and takes the fun out of storytelling. This is also helpful at building up a familiarity with telling the story of something when you want them to tell you what might have happened around a particular incident that day, but this is a secondary gain and shouldn't be your main motivation here.

Daytime camping: This is pitching a tent and allowing your child to camp outside in your garden for the day with a friend or their siblings. Give them some rations and encourage them to make food for each other out of what you give them (think about the makings of a basic sandwich and some mixed fruit and treats that they must work out how to divide and share fairly). They can pretend to be in the mountains and work out how to survive, or share stories or assign roles for what each person in the tent must do, such as find twigs, source water (from your tap is fine). By keeping it as a daytime activity you are not putting yourself through any stress of them sleeping outside alone at night.

This play supports children to become more autonomous and to explore their own passions and desires and to make choices independently of their parents while engaging with the world around them.

OBJECT PLAY

Object play should also be encouraged at this age and can be especially useful when your tween declares themselves too old for the symbolic play (though I wager they will embrace the camping and fort building). I like to introduce this with reference to myself by sharing a game I used to play as a child. I talk about how mobile phones were not part of my childhood and how phones used to be just fixed to the wall in your house and how we used to make our own phones to play with out of tin cans and string. Generally a child of this age scoffs or disbelieves this is possible, so we do it together.

Make telephones: Use two empty, washed tin cans without sharp edges or two paper cups and a ball of twine. Make a hole in the base of the tin cans and thread the twine through each, securing with a knot – ensure a lengthy distance between the two. You take one and have your child stand away from you so that the string is pulled tight. Take turns with one of you speaking into the tin can while the other places their can to their ear. *TIP:* this can be a nice way of sharing compliments or gratitude for each other or even initiating a tricky chat such as saying you were sad that something happened and so happy when something else happened. Invite them to share something similar back.

Make pom-pom people: Sit and teach your child how to make a wool pom-pom (I have described how to make these in the 15 Minutes of Nurture Play Ideas in the Introduction). For this activity have them make pairs of pom-poms and then show them how to glue them together and attach googly eye stickers to make pom-pom people. The child can play with them, exchange them, give them as gifts or turn them into decorations for Christmas or other celebration (use sparkly festive coloured wool for Christmas or black and orange wool for Halloween 'pumpkin' pom-poms).

Make paper snappers: This involves folding a square piece of paper a number of times in a particular folding sequence (watch this online) to make a snapper that opens and closes as you move your fingers in and out. You can put colours on the four corners on the outside, numbers on the eight sections inside and eight messages beneath that. You can theme these to be eight written competencies to compliment your child. You can use it creatively so that every time they whine that they are bored they take a chance on the snapper, turning up a chore or a treat. It can be creative discipline with eight creative consequences inside. The traditional method is for eight future predictions to be written in there.

This type of play encourages children to negotiate with others and work collaboratively to find out how to achieve a task. It also builds cooperation skills, and gaining mastery over such a task builds confidence.

Games with rules are really good for building and supporting emotional resilience in children as well. Part of being emotionally resilient is that you can internalise a set of rules and (mostly) stick to them. Children of this age are motivated to make sense of their world and to make sense of the rules their parents and other key adults (teachers/carers) impose on them, so rule-based play can be appealing. Games such as these:

Chasing: The person who is caught is now 'it' and must chase someone else to catch.

Tip the can/wall: One person is 'it' and all others hide. When called, the people hiding must take their moment to emerge and race the person who is on to tip the wall/can (bin) first. If the hidden person doesn't make it, they are now 'it'.

Statues: Play some music and everyone must dance, but they must all freeze completely when you pause the music. Walk among them to ensure no movements and if someone moves or giggles they are 'out' or simply swap and make them the person who is 'on' to avoid exclusion, if easier.

This type of play encourages skills such as turn-taking, coping with winning/losing, teamwork, being able to read cues in others and act on those, and problem-solving, all of which are vital for emotional resilience.

Emotional resilience really helps children to negotiate the stages of friendship formation. Most true friendships go through three key stages of development. There is the initial contact phase, when you first meet and are curious about each other. Then you have the interactive engagement stage whereby you are becoming more involved in each other's lives, know each other better and have found a common ground to connect on. This is a phase of acceptance and further exploration. The third stage is one of intimacy where the friendship is about knowing each other at a deeper and more emotional level. This is where you can read each other's non-verbal cues and might even develop a sense of 'knowing' how the other person is feeling or would feel about something. This is also a time for secret sharing or confiding in and being confided in. An intimate friendship can feel very special for both parties. This is a phase of deeper exploration.

Not all friendships will go through each of these phases (true of adult and child friendships) and that is okay. Indeed, most of us will have only a handful of the stage three intimate friendships in our lifetimes. Children of this age are often moving between stages one and two with their friendships, but towards the end of middle childhood you might see a stage three friendship emerge. Trust is central to intimate friendship formation, and as such a breach of trust between friends is very impactful on the relationship, as the friendship itself has been breached by the betrayal. In this regard, we do tend to see that girls of this age have fewer but more emotionally intense friendships than their male counterparts, who tend to be drawn towards larger group play that is more competitive and rule-oriented (team sports/designing and running their own sports league/tag/chasing, etc.).

Creating, forming and developing friendships are really important areas for children's development. They learn a lot about themselves and other people through their friendships, the highs and lows, the falling out and coming back together, the ruptures and the repair. That said, children do not need to have *lots* of friends, nor do they need to be popular. This might be a desire from a parent to see their child as popular with lots of friends as some kind of reassurance that all is well with them and that they are happy – or maybe we have some of our unresolved feelings about popularity that are projected outwards too (this is not a judgement but an opportunity for reflection). Actually, many children are happiest with a couple of good friends and may even prefer smaller groups of three children. Your child being happy is the cue that you are looking for. If they have a couple of friends and are happy and engaged and talking about those friends, then take it that all is well and they have no need for more friendships right now. (I say a couple of friends, as in two, because having one good friend can be challenging if that child is absent from school and your child feels they have no one else to connect with that day or play with outside.)

And remember, as best you can, as much as you can, where you can, stay out of your child's friendships and afford them the important space to work it out. There will only be rare occasions where you have to step in to address an issue that requires an adult's input.

I absolutely do not wish to minimise or trivialise the important role adults, especially parents, play in the lives of children *but* there are areas of our children's development that can be clouded by our more adult-centric outlook and this is one of them. Children are biologically wired to grow up in a culture of childhood and other children, namely their peers, are central to this development. We parents play a very important role in supporting, guiding and shaping our children across all phases of development but we should be as much led and influenced by them as they are by us. The parent–child relationship is a dance of synchrony, and knowing when to lead and when to follow, when to change the tune to elicit a different dance and when to step out and let a new dance partner take a whirl are all vital to our children's healthy emotional and psychosocial development. If you trust yourself as a parent, you can trust your child to form and develop relationships for themselves that are quite outside you and the parent–child relationship. This is a phase of childhood where the goal is to enhance and increase your child's independence. Your child will grow in independence when they grow in courage, so that they can face and handle challenges that will come their way, so let them try, fail, learn, try again, succeed and grow as confident, courageous, independent and resilient beings. This is important groundwork now, hence why I am labouring this point, as it really helps them (and you) to prepare for adolescence.

15-MINUTE PARENTING TIP TO SUPPORT YOUR CHILD'S FRIENDSHIPS IF AND WHEN NEEDED

If you have a child who can struggle when they have a friend over at your house to really let the friend 'in' to their play and environment, you can start them off with a simple baking activity whereby you have them mix ingredients you have laid out. They go and play without you while the buns (for example) bake and cool down. Bring them back together to decorate the buns towards the end of the play date. This can be a nice way of structuring the beginning and end of the play date (if it needs that help) and affords them free play together in the middle.

BRINGING BACK THE BOOKS

Children of this age have a pronounced sense of justice and fairness, of right and wrong, so it stands to reason that these themes emerge in their play. It is not unusual to observe children play out themes of good and bad – those who do wrong get discovered and punished and those who do right win the day. There is a reason that this is central to the themes of children's books.

Reading is such a great way to keep a playful, creative and imaginative relationship with your child at this age. And if they don't like to read books, find something they will read, such as a comic book, and be interested in what interests them.

C.S. Lewis suggested that *we read to know that we are not alone.* Children need to know where they are going and how they will get there, and they can do this through books, not screens.

Never assume that children, being young and small, have small feelings and experiences of the world they live in. This is simply not true and a good story, one that is truly written for the child reader, leads a child to say the otherwise unsayable. Books are a safe way to be scared and to explore what scares us because being afraid while knowing everything will somehow be okay is powerful for children. Books for children are not afraid to explore dark themes. Everything does not always end well and there can be a truth in the sadness for children to learn. Reading builds the fabric of our children's brains.

Stories, of course, are more than books. Storytelling is ever evolving, from the Seanachaí to story sacks to story cubes. (Seanachaí, pronounced shan-a-key, is a traditional Gaelic story-teller, common in Irish and Scottish cultures. The word means *bearer of old lore* and their role was to keep track of important events, stories, even laws, family genealogy and more. They kept the stories of the past alive for next generations, and it is now a recognised art form.)

If literacy is a challenge in your home, for you or your child, there are other ways to bring storytelling into your child's life and to use this to enhance your relationship. One such way is creating a story sack together.

A story sack is a large cloth bag (I use a pillow case tied with some ribbon) containing your child's favourite book with support-ing materials to stimulate language activities and make reading a memorable and enjoyable experience.

Example – *Harry Potter and the Philosopher's Stone*
by J.K. Rowling

Include the following in your story sack:

- Copy of the book – if the child has literacy issues perhaps you listened to the audiobook and that is fine of course, but I still always include a copy of the physical book so that it can be touched and flicked through.
- Models (finger puppets or Lego/Playmobil style characters are fine) of the children, adults, witches/wizards if you can get them – always keep an eye open in the charity shops where people donate their unwanted toys as I have sourced some great pieces for this kind of thing in such places over the years.
- Props: A witch/wizard's hat, a cape and a wand or stick that can represent one (Halloween is the season to stock up on these things), a small bowl with small tubs of water, sand, coloured sand or glitter, herbs that smell strongly (such as cinnamon/ginger/curry). This is to allow them to mix a potion as if they were a student at Hogwarts. Ensure that there is at least a hat for you to wear to join in with them. Have fun making up some spells with this part and deepen their experience by wondering what spells they would cast if they had magic powers and what they would wish for themselves and for someone else they know.
- A magic card trick or some other simple magic trick they can learn to do (joke/novelty shops tend to have things like these or simply include a coin and look up online how to do a card or coin trick yourself that you can now teach them).
- Paper and crayons – to draw your favourite bits. Decide what bits you would delete and change and what would you add.

You 'tell' the story by playing it out together, and the other props are there to deepen your child's understanding and engagement with the main themes of the book. This is a perfectly valid way of telling a story together when reading may not be available for you. It is also a very effective way to engage them at a more imaginative level in exploring some themes that have emerged from a book they/you are reading and to deepen their understanding and awareness of such matters.

Story cubes/storytelling dice (mentioned earlier) are another great way to do this. You just role the storytelling dice and however they land use the symbols facing upwards to tell a story together. Or get some fuzzy felt and boards and mix up all the pieces (some fuzzy felt sets come in set story/theme sets so I tend to buy a few and then mix up all of the pieces so that the child can project onto the felt and tell their own story) and build a picture that allows you to sit together and develop a story around what you created together.

A reluctant reader can still be engaged if you set a challenge that you will both read the same book at the same time, one chapter per night, and the next day you have to 'test' each other's recollections by coming up with two questions to ask each other about that chapter. Keep it playful though – there is no consequence for getting it wrong. You can also read a book together and at the end discuss how it ended and if they were the author, how they might change the ending. Talk it out, draw it and write the new ending.

Join a library and go there once a week. If your child is a reluctant reader, simply allow them to see you take and return books in a place where there are so many books. Linger to see if they will browse or show some interest and don't comment on that, just let it happen. Let them know that they have their own library card if they ever want to borrow a book themselves.

But where possible, get them reading and keep them reading.

From the beginning of stories and fairy tales in particular there have been inherent cautions and warnings that serve as a behavioural code for children. What is *Little Red Riding Hood* if not a cautionary tale dissuading us from straying from the path of duty in pursuit of our desire in case we get devoured for doing so? Of course, it is also an important story that helps children understand that they shouldn't talk to strangers. *The Princess and the Frog* can be read as a reminder that not everything, or indeed everyone, is as we might initially see it and people are more than how they look (lots of fairy tales have this message in their narratives).

Many fairy tales have been cleansed by their Disneyfication but I would strongly encourage you to read, especially to your children in middle childhood, the original Grimm's brothers versions with their darker and much more intriguing tone. Stories and books in particular are a step removed from the child and their own narrative and as such provide a great way for them to explore difficult and dark themes and gain learning and lessons for their own lives.

CHAPTER 3

Sibling Relationships in Middle Childhood

The sibling relationship is likely to last longer than other relationships your children will have throughout their lives. A lot of research has been conducted into the long-term life outcomes for children who grow up with siblings[2] and what all of the research tends to highlight is that while the sibling relationship will most likely be the longest relationship your child has, it is also a unique type of relationship in anyone's life for other reasons.

Key characteristics that account for the quality of sibling relationships are the emotional tone of the relationship: the level of warmth they feel and show each other; the level of involvement in each other's life, i.e. the amount of time they spend together; and ambivalence, i.e. how they actually get on together.

TESTING THE EMOTIONAL TEMPERATURE

Let me start with the **emotional tone** of the relationship. The sibling relationship is probably the most uninhibited relationship your children will have in their lives. Because of this lack of inhibition, they have increased influence on each other in terms of how each thinks, feels and ultimately behaves. You can support the emotional tone of their relationship by increasing their empathic awareness of each other. *Wondering* is a great way to do this. You can wonder how each imagines the other might be feeling about a given situation. I like to approach this in a *role reversal* way whereby I listen to each child's side of the argument and, without comment, I then ask them to tell me the same story but from their sibling's point of view. The challenge here is that they cannot interject with their own justifications and must tell the story start to finish, as they perceive the other's perspective to be. Then I wonder how they feel about it and how their sibling might be feeling and what action now would change both children's feelings. Give it a go as it really is a nice way to support your children without getting pulled in to resolve things for them and also increases their empathy for each other and their critical-thinking abilities.

Think about the *amount of time* your children spend in each other's company, even if that is simply sitting in close proximity not directly engaging with each other. It might surprise you to realise that by middle childhood your children spend more time with and around each other than they do with you, their parents.[3] But, of course, the length of time they are around each other is only half of the story here because what matters within this time is the level of involvement they have with each other. Positive and socially engaged interaction will be a more positive variable than simply sitting close by while ignoring each other. It is important here that you facilitate play that offers opportunities for shared joy. This involves activities such as (though of course not limited to) those listed in the next section.

15-minute play to bring siblings together

A scavenger hunt around your home or garden: Hide something – this can be a privilege rather than a thing, i.e. the treasure to be found might be the Wi-Fi code or the ingredients to bake cookies with you or a time voucher to use to stay up a bit later on Friday nights. Set them cryptic clues that they must work out together. Ensure you play to each child's strengths on the clues so that each one has something to contribute and they need each other to achieve the task.

Hand them a box of mixed **Lego** and remove the instruction manual so that they have to work together to build the item.

Set a **word-free hour** and tell them they can only communicate with facial expressions. I like this as it teaches them to read each other's non-verbal cues and emotional responses, which is valuable when they are engaged in conflict with each other or simply not aware of the effect they are having on each other. Increase the fun by joining in yourself here.

Play **pass the touch/non-verbal:** Simply pass a smile or a wink to each other and remember if you start sending it one way, reverse the order so that everyone gives and receives from each other. Equally, draw a shape or symbol or number on one back with your finger and have the recipient draw it on the next person's back as they felt it. It's fun to see how it ends up and these games work especially well if you have three or more children to play it with together. You can add in a round using verbal phrases but structure this so that they must pass a compliment around – something about a behaviour, but not an appearance-based compliment.

Take a large blanket, place a balloon on it and ask everyone to hold a part and lift it up. Now call one name at a time and you must all work together to tilt and dip and lift the blanket to ensure the balloon is sent to the named person. Keeping the balloon in the centre, play **hot potato cold potato –** every time you say hot potato you all vigorously shake and lift the balloon up, making sure you catch it with the blanket each time; cold potato means you softly shake and lift. This is great for bringing everyone's energies up/down and co-regulating together.

COLLABORATIVE CHALLENGE PLAY

This leads us to how they actually get on. The sibling relationship is marked by ambivalence – they can be each other's best friends and worst enemies rolled into one and this juxtaposition increases the emotional charge in the relationship. To support them in negotiating this ambivalence, try to blend in some collaborative challenge play. Challenge is an inherent part of the sibling relationship so why not make this ambivalence work for you by positively reframing it into something they can work out together?

Cotton-ball games: Place one cotton ball on a tabletop and challenge them to keep it moving for as long as possible without it falling off the table – and without touching it with their hands. To achieve this, they will have to bend down to the same level and blow the cotton ball calmly over and back between them, taking turns, perhaps working out that if they held hands around the edge of the surface they would create a barrier to prevent the cotton ball from falling off (while holding hands – bonus!). By making the challenge about keeping it on the table you eliminate the competitive goal-scoring tendency that could creep in otherwise. Increase the challenge here to make it more engaging for longer, especially for the older children in this age group, by adding in two or three cotton balls and now they must manage to keep all three on the table, meaning they have to keep an eye on more than one thing at the same time.

Another way to try this would be to make a track with masking tape on a hard-surfaced floor. Place a cotton ball at one end and give both children a (paper) straw. One child can sit at the opposite end of the track. Now one of them starts blowing the cotton ball up the track while their sibling encourages them. The motivation is that by encouraging their sibling to do well, they will get their turn. You can increase the challenge here by saying that if the cotton ball comes out of the track they must go back to the start, and by making the track narrower at certain points or adding in a zigzag or roundabout. (**Note:** Only increase the level of challenge when you know that they can manage it; typically, the older they are, the more challenge I add in.)

Scatter a handful of cotton balls around the room and challenge them to pick all of them up in a set time. You can use a large sand timer (a five-minute one might be good here and use plenty of cotton balls around the space). The challenge here is that they must pick up each cotton ball one at a time with their bare foot and hop it back over to a basket in the corner of the room. They must work together to clear the floor in the allotted time.

Using challenge in a positive way to encourage them to work together and support each other is a creative way to teach them to better cope with the inherent ambivalence in the sibling relationship.

Just because your children at this stage of development are spending more time with each other than they are with you doesn't mean that parents are not a huge influence in the sibling relationship, because you are. The research highlights how it is parenting behaviour that is often modelled in the sibling relationship, marking a significant overlap in the quality of parent–child relationship and sibling relationship. If there are problems in the parent–child relationship we tend to see problems in the sibling relationship too. If you focus on changing, improving, strengthening and enhancing your relationship with each of your children you are also supporting the strengthening and enhancement of their relationship with each other – *a small change that can make a big difference.*

In my consultations with parents I always start with the same questions and I invite you to pause right now and work through these questions in the list below.

QUICK PARENT–CHILD RELATIONSHIP CHECK-IN

1. When did you first realise that you loved your child?
2. Do you still love your child?
3. How does thinking about that make you feel?
4. Who in your life (past or present) does your child remind you of?
5. How do you feel about *that* person?

I say it a lot, but honestly there is no better way to discover your own unresolved emotional issues than to have a child. Becoming a parent will bring all of your stuff, including stuff you didn't even know you had buried, screaming to the surface. And this can often get played out in our relationships with our children, whereby we (unconsciously) displace aspects of another relationship in our lives onto the relationship with the child who reminds us of that other person. Becoming the parent of a child is, of course, going to replay aspects of our time being the child of our parent.

We can displace both positive and negative feelings from our past relationships onto our relationships with our children. So it is important to reflect and answer the above questions relating to each of your children individually. If you find yourself idealising one child and perhaps not 'demonising' but being tougher on another child, take time to reflect inwards as to why that might be and what it is telling you about yourself.

Identifying our own emotional baggage can be transformative not only for us personally but also in terms of how we relate to our children, and also for them, in terms of how they relate to each other. Understanding our own triggers allows us to better understand what is activated within us and where our frustration is really coming from before we spill it out onto our children.

This being said, please also bear in mind that *when* not *if* (because it definitely will happen to all of us) we do lose it with our children, we can make repair and apologise. Explain that we shouted because we felt frustrated with their behaviour but not with them. It is important to model healthy rupture followed by repair for our children.

SIBLING RIVALRY

Sibling rivalry is developmentally normal, though not pleasant to parent through. It is something that parents contact me about regularly as a source of worry, especially concerning the best ways to intervene. Sibling rows are frequent and mostly poorly resolved, which can leave a trace of simmering tension ready to spark off the next time they row, and can become highly aggressive (physically and/or verbally). I suggest a flexible and creative approach to intervention because in these situations it is so important that you do not allow yourself to get pulled *into* the tension as adjudicator or referee. There is a fine line between stepping in and sorting out whatever is happening, thereby running the risk of depriving children of the opportunity to learn how to resolve conflict for themselves, and not intervening at all, which may mean the tension escalates and the situation can become more physical or harmful. Perhaps try mediating your children's conflicts rather than adjudicating them.

So how might you attempt to achieve this? Try this *facilitated listening* technique.

Game to support listening to others

Separate the children from the situation and convene at a neutral space, perhaps in the sitting room or around the kitchen table. Now focus on facilitating a dialogue whereby each party gets to speak uninterrupted about how they see the situation and how they feel. After child A has spoken, reflect back what they have said *without* commenting on the accuracy or adding in any of your own thoughts or feelings on the matter. Now child B gets to speak from their point of view and again you reflect back what you have heard them say.

This process allows you to repeat their narrative so the other child gets to hear it twice and also affords the speaking child an opportunity to clarify any of it. Your role here is to facilitate the dialogue/negotiation but you leave the final resolution up to them, asking, 'Okay, so what do you think needs to happen next for us to move on?' (**Note:** If your children are in the older age bracket of middle childhood, 10–12 years old, you can ask each of them to do the reflecting back what they have heard their sibling say *without* commenting on the accuracy of their sibling's version. This is a good opportunity to practise reflective listening skills with your children as well. This process may not take as long to mediate and you are improving the outcome of their conflict while enabling them to develop better conflict resolution and empathy skills.)

When it comes to consequences for sibling rivalry, which I view as a normal phase of everybody's development, stay creative and keep in mind what you are hoping to achieve as an outcome. This could be an end to the immediate tension and reminding them how they actually like a whole lot more about each other than they dislike.

TEAMWORK – 15 MINUTES OF COLLABORATIVE PLAY

Have them work on something together, be that a chore for you or something creative such as working out a jigsaw puzzle together or writing each other a card that states something they appreciate about the other. If they assert that they do not appreciate anything about the other, it will simply take them longer to achieve this but that is on them and within their control. You could also make the consequence that they each must think of something kind to do for the other *that day* – it should be that day because consequences should be quick and allow everyone to move on rather than let things fester.

Pay attention to the tasks you see them enjoy doing together, such as gaming, baking, arts and crafts, watching a movie they both like, playing football, trampolining, dancing, drawing/painting, making slime. These are the tasks you will want to redirect them towards once the conflict at hand has been resolved because it allows them to engage in repair in a *doing* rather than a *saying* way. Siblings will fight, but reminding them of how they also enjoy each other can ensure that there is enough of a balance between sibling warmth and conflict, which will certainly help counteract any long-term impact on their sibling relationship as they grow and develop into adulthood. I'm quite sure that many of us can step back and recall how as children we wanted to kill our siblings but as adults we would kill for them (figuratively speaking of course).

All children want our undivided love and attention at various times. We can feel ourselves pulled in every direction trying to meet everyone's needs as we attempt to be 'fair' and give them all the same amount of our time and focus. However, what is truly fair is that everyone gets as much as they need to grow and develop in a healthy way. And that will look different for each different child, even within the one family. Rather than think about having a favourite child, consider that you may well have a child you find easier and more fun to parent than another. Be aware of how much time and attention you willingly bestow on them and how it might well be an effort to give something similar to another child. That is not remotely to infer that you do not love each child, as loving them and finding one easier than another to connect with are not the same thing at all. In order to keep the balance on fair and equitable treatment for all children, you could consider developing house/family rules that apply to everyone, modified in accordance to each one's age/stage of development/ability. House rules and family expectations should be applied equally to everyone in the family. Expecting everyone to try *their* best, contribute *their* piece, pull *their* weight and be true to who *they* are within your family is equitable and balanced. How this looks for everyone won't be exactly the same but what matters is that your parental expectation is the same for everyone, that is everyone doing *their* part to the best of *their* ability. That is how to stay 'fair'.

It may sound counter-intuitive to say that in order to be fair you should treat your children differently but isn't this because they are all different? Children I meet with talk about how frustrating it is for them when they perceive a sibling is trying to compete with them for what they see is *their* place within the family. I think that this is one of the main triggers for sibling disharmony.

Lucy (ten years old) was attending with me because her parents had grown very concerned about how they perceived her to be withdrawing from the family with increasing angry outbursts, her aggression largely directed towards her younger sister (eight years old). They identified that the girls had always bickered but this had mostly been manageable until the spring of this year (I saw Lucy in the autumn so it had been escalating for approximately six months). They described Lucy as a high-achieving, sporty and popular girl with plenty of friends who enjoyed school and her extracurricular activities. She was an avid athlete in her local running club, something she had been doing for four years now, having become interested after watching the London Olympics. She was serious and competitive.

When I met Lucy I experienced her as closed and defensive. She knew why she was coming to me. (I had been very open with her about what her parents had shared with me about her and her life and invited her to correct any of that information from her point of view – I always do this with children I meet to ensure I am transparent and trustworthy for them.) I could see that a top-down approach (starting with the neo-cortex thinking/reasoning/logical part of the brain) such as talk therapy was not going to work so I switched to what we call a bottom-up approach (doing the communication rather than saying it). We used a variety of creative, narrative-based techniques that enabled her to tell her story without actually sitting down and speaking it directly to me. I provided a gently reflective observation of what she was doing (sand-tray work, art, clay, story cubes) and one day she sat back, sighed and exclaimed, 'I hate that THEY let HER ruin running for me.'

This enabled Lucy to speak about how she had valued running as 'her thing' in their family, saw herself as the good runner and really developed this as part of her identity. Her parents saw how good this had been for her confidence and self-esteem and social-skills development so naturally thought it would be nice to also have her sister participate and benefit similarly. The problem arose when Lucy saw that her younger sister was especially good at running and was aware that others were commenting on how fast she was. She felt usurped and this prompted a head-to-head conflict between her and her sister whereby she felt there could only be one winner, one 'best runner'.

Part of the solution here was to support Lucy to redefine the nature of her conflict and extract and process her fear that she was not good enough unless she was the best at something. She was not simply angry, she was fearful and anxious.

Understanding what emotional states actually underpin our overt behaviours is essential in working through a more positive way of being together. With the family, we worked on **collaborative challenge-based play** *that celebrated efforts over outcomes; we explored* **opportunities for shared joy** *between the girls and highlighted what they shared in common rather than what separated them. This was about retaining a sense of self for Lucy while defining a new type of relationship with her sister and parents.*

For the **collaborative challenge-based play** *we played balloon relay and balloon between bodies.*

Balloon relay: *Taking a blown-up balloon, I had the two girls stand side by side and placed the balloon between their shoulders. We had their mum/dad stand at the opposite end of the room and on their cue the girls had to walk/run with the balloon up to the parent, high five them, turn around and walk/ run the balloon back to the starting place, without touching the balloon with their hands or dropping it. We increased the level of challenge here by having the girls bring the balloon up to their parents and transfer the balloon from their bodies to their parents without anyone touching it with their hands, and then their parents walked it back to the starting place before returning and transferring it back to the girls.*

Balloon between bodies *worked really well here as it called for the two girls to stand in close physical proximity and stay close enough without getting right into each other's personal space because if you stand too close the balloon will burst; not close enough means the balloon will fall. We placed the balloon tummy to tummy so that the girls were facing each other and their parents directed them to move in synchrony up and down, side to side and turning around. The trick was that they could not touch the balloon with their hands and had to ensure it did not fall.* (***Tip:*** *increase the level of touch here by having the children place their hands up against each other's. This ensures touch, eye contact, connection and collaboration. We moved the balloon up between foreheads, raised arms, knees to knees, etc. too.)*

*As we observed the fun coming back into their relationship I wondered if we could support them to experience **further relationship repair through nurture**. To this end I introduced both girls to a mini-spa experience at home. They immersed their hands in a basin of warm (nice-smelling) soapy water. I wondered if they could place both hands flat at the end of the basin and still manage to touch the tips of each other's fingers. I wondered if they could keep their hands flat yet tangle or entwine their fingers (a little challenge with a lot of nurture). We had them do a hand-stack in the basin of water. We had them scoop a handful of bubbles up and pass these from one girl's hand to the other's, scraping the bubbles to each other over and back to see how long it took for the bubbles to disappear. We had them pat dry each other's hands in a nice soft hand towel and rub lotion into each other's hands. Then, with some help from the parents, they painted each other's nails and lightly blew on each other's fingers to help them dry.*

This doing rather than saying interactive repair experience really strengthened and enhanced their relationship. I am not going to say it prevented any further rivalry or conflict, but it lessened the intensity of these experiences and certainly helped to move Lucy out of the state of envy she had become locked into. When a sibling is no longer experienced as a threat to one child's sense of self, they are freed up to support and even enjoy each other's company, at least most of the time. Mild to moderate levels of sibling rivalry and conflict/tension can be quite normal and even a good opportunity for children to learn about conflict resolution and solution-focused critical thinking skills.

Ideally parents should explore opportunities for celebrating each of their children for their unique qualities and individual interests. This could mean that they each have hobbies or extracurricular activities that are about them and what they like and are good at. It really only becomes an issue when, as above in this case study, the siblings share the hobby/interest and competitive conflict emerges in the relationship. We are trying to encourage our children to be supportive of one another by avoiding direct competition and comparison.

What I have been writing about is in the range of normal sibling rivalry and how it can directly impact on children's emotional growth and development or family relations. However, if the conflict between siblings becomes overtly aggressive and crosses a line from what could possibly be considered normal into more physically and/or verbally abusive behaviour, a parent must always step in and take action to keep themselves and other children safe. If you observe that one of your children tends to, repeatedly and in a focused and threatening manner, exert control or dominance over their sibling(s), perhaps by threatening parental consequences on your behalf ('If you don't do what I say I'll tell Mum/Dad on you and they won't let you go to your friend's party this weekend'), you should treat it seriously and ensure that you intervene with firm boundaries and monitor the situation. If your creative and then direct parental intervention does not divert the behaviour described here, you should consider seeking support from a suitably trained and qualified child mental-health professional who can provide support via therapeutic parenting and/or child psychotherapy services.

CHAPTER 4

Difficult Conversations (the Ones That Catch You off Guard and Keep You on Your Toes!)

Middle childhood is a time when children have to face some of life's more difficult topics, temptations and realisations that force them to confront the fact that they are not as in control of their world as they once thought they might be. This is a tough time for them but it can also be tough for parents to support them through this phase and to be ready for the difficult conversations. This chapter explores some of the main ones that I come across in my work with families, though of course this is not intended to be an exhaustive list.

LET'S TALK ABOUT SEX

By the upper end of this middle-childhood stage (11–12 years old typically – there will always be someone to buck this trend so attend and attune to where your child is developmentally rather than chronologically) children might start dropping in terms like boyfriend/girlfriend or you may overhear snippets between them and their friends as to who *fancies* who. There may even be some first kisses creeping in at 12 years old or soon after. Most of these, at least the early ones, are flirtatious fantasy-based explorations, something to imagine and talk about with friends. But there is no harm in starting the conversation now before more intense and active intimate attachments develop.

It is important that you keep the lines of communication open and that you start to embrace that very fine balance between being *interested* versus *intrusive* in their lives. You don't want to blow it out of proportion by taking it far too seriously, but at the same time do not take this as an opportunity to poke fun at their feelings or for having boyfriends/girlfriends. If we embarrass them about their feelings they will likely retreat further away from us.

Think back to your own feelings and first crushes – how do you wish people had responded to you? Start from that point.

You might know their crushes to be innocent and fantasy-based and something to talk about with their friends, but you should also note this new awareness of and interest in having a relationship also marks the start of being interested in their own sexuality and desire. So this is the time to grow your sex-talk up a bit more. I say time to grow your talk up as I am hoping that you have been talking about bodies from their toddlerhood stage of development (using correct names for body parts) and touch (who can touch who and when and where one can touch oneself), gradually including where babies come from and then body changes and things like menstruation and wet dreams (nocturnal emissions, to give them their formal title). It is always easier if this is a topic that has been a part of your relationship with your child so that you can simply grow the content up as needed rather than start introducing a difficult topic at the most difficult age to do so.

When it comes to talking with your children about sex, it pays to think through what you want to say and how you will say it in advance. A little tip here is to practise saying it aloud with your partner (helpful at ensuring you stay on the same page in terms of what you will say) or a friend/family member. Hearing yourself say something is not the same as thinking it. It also allows you to get any awkwardness or tripping over the words out of the way before you speak with your children. Now, if you are reading this and shrugging, thinking you don't find this awkward at all, that is fantastic *but* just because you are super comfortable with speaking about sex doesn't mean your pre-teen will be. So be sensitive to how they are experiencing what you are saying and perhaps modify how you say it to make it more manageable for them.

Keep the content direct, factual and take regular pauses to check in with them as to how they are receiving the information; allow them to ask questions as you go. This will ensure a deeper understanding of what you are saying but will also allow you to spot if they are becoming overwhelmed by it. As puberty will arrive for many (even most) children by the end of this middle-childhood phase, ensure that you talk about breasts, new hair growth, periods and wet dreams, and normalise it while respecting how embarrassing it might be for them. Talk openly about sexual intercourse and use anatomically correct language. How you speak about sex will be influenced and framed by your own moral code and that is perfectly fine once you ensure that you are sticking to facts within that framework. Any conversation about sex should include contraception and consent as a part of the narrative.

At this point, you might well be thinking, *Yeah, yeah that all sounds great, Joanna, but* **how** *do I cover all of that in an appropriate way for my pre-teen?* I understand that and I also hate reading advice that sounds wonderful in theory but there is no practical application included. So, what follows is my *suggestion* of a conversation that includes all of this. Please read and modify in accordance with your moral beliefs, your own knowledge of your child's developmental capacity and how comfortable you are. This could be one conversation or three conversations, depending on all of those variables. As I said, it is just a suggestion and not intended to be a script.

Sex is something people share together when they are old enough, much older than you are right now. People have sex to make a baby together but also have sex because it feels really nice for grown-ups. Sex can be between people who are in a relationship together or sometimes between people who might not know each other all that well. That's okay but what's really important is that everyone says yes to having sex before it happens and that everyone is happy to keep saying yes while it's happening. It's okay to say no or to say yes and then change your mind to a no at any time, and that 'no' must be listened to and respected. It's never ever okay to force someone to have sex or to do anything sexual that they're not 100 per cent happy to do. To say yes and mean it, everyone involved must be sober and have a clear enough mind to make that choice, so if someone is really drunk or sleepy because they've taken some medication or just gone to bed for the night, no one should ever try to have sex with them.

Staying healthy is also an important part of sex, so using contraception is especially important. Some contraception stops you getting pregnant and some also stops anyone getting a sexually transmitted infection. There are lots of choices about that so when you're older and thinking about having sex please do come to me so that we can talk about it and make sure you're as safe as you need to be. Remember, the most important thing about sex is that you wait until you feel fully ready, you trust the person you're having sex with, you check that they're happy to have sex and then are happy to keep having sex even when you've started because sex should be something fun for everyone involved. You always stay safe and use protection-based contraception. I want you to know that you can always come to talk to me about this.

This kind of narrative may well be enough for some children and some will want you to explain in detail what a sexually transmitted infection is and what exactly happens in sex (the 'what goes where' conversation). Perhaps you answer these questions now or perhaps you say something like, 'Those are great questions. I think we've talked enough about it for now but we can talk about those questions and any others the next time we get to sit together and have this chat.' I tend to encourage parents to answer the questions that are asked of you within any given topic and be careful of flooding them with details they haven't yet sought out. Start by checking what they already know or think about sex (this may surprise you) and take that as a starting point.

An added note on this one. It is really important to have boundaries for this type of conversation and remind your child that it is not their job to tell their friends about this topic – it is the job of parents to do that. Remind them that this goes for their younger siblings too, as you will make sure that they know as much as they need to.

MANAGING ECO-ANXIETY IN YOUR CLIMATE-CHANGE CONVERSATIONS

A somewhat new yet increasing topic is that of **climate change** and associated **eco-anxiety.** This is about finding a way of talking about climate change without scaring your children, although let's acknowledge that this is a scary topic. As with any fear a child expresses, we should take it seriously and not seek to dismiss or minimise it. I do believe that when we do this it comes from a place of not wanting our children to feel scared or overwhelmed. However, some fears are valid and the best way to teach children to handle these fears better is to allow them to think, feel and process their way out of them *with* you.

I am coming across this issue more and more, whereas even five years ago this would not have featured on my highlights list. This is not to say climate change wasn't an issue five years ago – it most certainly was – but it wasn't such a dominant part of our social and political discourse as it now is. A mistake often made by adults is to assume that children won't understand the complexity of such subjects or will feel disempowered and not able to do anything about them. Involving our children in social change is the best solution to this; however, it calls on us to think hard about how we will approach such topics within our parenting.

The best way to start a conversation with children about climate change is to lay the groundwork in a positive and accessible way. This helps to develop an appreciation for nature and why the earth is worth protecting before you start talking about climate change and what it means. Here are some things you could do together:

- Watch nature documentaries together and discuss what you see.
- Visit animal sanctuaries together and discuss what you see.
- Take regular walks along the coast/beach/in forests or in parks and other local green spaces, point out everything around you and talk about what you see.
- Involve your children in gardening and consider a wild-flower patch that will encourages bees to visit.
- Visit your local farmers' market together.
- Walk and cycle weekly and talk about why doing so is good for the planet.
- Commit to micro changes at home such as recycling, composting and a reduce, reuse, recycle model. Ensure that you keep your child actively involved in these activities.
- Focus on developing skills and solutions that your child can be actively involved in. What can you do at home, in your community, at school? Maybe support your child in writing to your local government representatives and ask what action plan the government has on these issues. Support your child in participating in safe and organised protests. Sit with them and watch talks and interviews with

youth activists to ensure they feel empowered as a young citizen to make a difference.

One 10-year-old boy shared his views with me on this topic. He was talking about how worried he was about our planet and that adults weren't taking climate change seriously. We reflected on this but also on what he felt he could do to help adults better understand this topic. I invited him to explain it to me to practise how he might do this. He told me that the earth was getting too hot because we had left the winter duvet on it when we should switch to a lighter tog summer duvet that would help it cool down. I told him that made a lot of sense to me and he moved on to some practical things we could all do to lighten the duvet.

It is always best to go with your child's interest rather than introducing a topic they are not engaged with. Because climate change is so important it is well worth stimulating their interest in the topic to ensure that they are informed and not scared when they start to be exposed to this. Ideally, you would start this process as early as possible and grow the conversation up with them as they get older – but it is never too late to start.

Of course, you must also inform yourself so that you can inform your children but even on this I would add a caveat. It is okay and even valuable to admit to your child that you are also feeling overwhelmed and a bit scared by all of the coverage and suggest that you do some research together so that you take each other on a journey of learning in this regard. Link in with climate-change groups and non-governmental organisations in your local area and ask them for resources or to meet with you and your children to discuss the matter further. Many of these have resources developed specifically to support parents in discussing this topic with their children. They can also help ensure that you are turning to fact-based resources. Remember, you don't need to give scientific-level explanations but be open to shared learning and have a decent grasp of key concepts. It can also be useful to link in with your school and see how they will be addressing the topic as part of the curriculum so that you stay on message and draw on their content as support.

Staying focused on solutions and showing excitement, enthusiasm and curiosity about positive actions you can take goes a long way to counteracting the anxiety and fear the subject matter can stir up in this age group.

VIDEO GAMING – IMPACT ON LANGUAGE AND BEHAVIOUR

Children's play in this stage of middle childhood becomes less about play activities and more about playing online or in a more structured less imaginative way in general (bikes, sports, etc.). My advice on online gaming is to get interested in what interests your child. It is a way to stay connected, but always remember that line between intrusive and interested. Say something like, 'I love to see how much you enjoy your online gaming. I don't know much about that type of play, so can you teach me a game you like to play with friends? Maybe I can add a headset and listen in to what interactive gaming is like while you play. I'll just listen and won't distract you and we can talk about it afterwards.'

The main questions I get asked about online gaming are to do with its effect on children's behaviour and emotional well-being. The answer is that there is no clear-cut answer on this one as no two children are the same or will cope and respond in the same way. Some children at this age manage online gaming really well; they can play the game, come offline when done and get on with their activities and interactions. Other children this age have a tendency to become hyper-aroused by online gaming and really struggle to transition offline again, resulting in rage and aggressive outbursts that can become very problematic to manage with and for them. You will have to judge this based on your knowledge of your own child, but a good general rule is no more than 30–40 minutes of online gaming time without at least a solid 15-minute interruption to engage in the real world. Everything pauses these days so get them to pause and come do something with you for 15 minutes. Something a little sensory based is useful here as it re-engages them in that all important *doing not saying* way while approaching their highly stimulated brains from the bottom (brain stem) up rather than asking them to meet you in a cognitive, verbal, logic and reasoning way (neo-cortex or top of brain down). Consider something like asking them to wash some carrots and potatoes for you to help with dinner prep. The washing of the vegetables is a sensory and tactile activity and after a few minutes you can gently start to chat (not question but just talk about anything at all) with them and secure that connection before they go back online to finish their game or the allotted time you give them.

All of this being said, please be mindful as to what type of game/interactive gaming activities your children are engaged in. Certain video games carry age restrictions with good reason, as the content, graphics and themes contained in them are intended to be viewed and accessed by adult gamers not young children. What follows is a case study that shows how younger children will struggle to manage adult themes that they are simply not mature enough to fully grasp.

Laura aged 10 years came to see me with her mother. I (as always) had met with her mother before this session (I do this so that parents can meet me, ask any questions of me and share with me any relevant details about their child I might need to know ahead of time). In this parent-intake session, Laura's mother had shared with me what she knew to have happened but that she didn't know what to do about it or how to help Laura through it.

I was aware that her mother was distressed about what had happened herself so we spent some time talking it through and reflecting on her own feelings about it. Laura played with some boys the same age locally and had done since being in preschool together. While in one of their homes, one of the boys had suggested that Laura be taken to a bedroom by another boy so he could 'do sex to her'. Laura had been frightened and had left the house and come home upset, telling her mother what had taken place. Her mother had comforted her and said that the boys were being silly and should not have said that and she was right to leave and tell her. A few weeks later while on a group outing, another of these boys said to Laura and some other girls that sex is what boys do to girls and then they pay them and kill them.

Again, this caused Laura a great deal of distress and she said she no longer wanted to play with these boys she had always been friends with. It transpired that these boys were all playing a particular 18-certified video game that contained themes of sex workers being paid for sex and beaten up and/or killed. These boys had normalised this as a behaviour that was not only socially acceptable to speak about but was something that would be expected of them. I do not think that they were consciously seeking to scare or distress Laura but were simply telling her how it is between boys and girls.

I focused on supporting Laura to process this distressing experience and on helping her mother to find a way to meet with the parents of one of the boys she had the best relationship with, share what had happened and make them aware of the impact of this video game. I am not naming the game, though many of you will know which one it is, but it is important to note that the game is an adult game and not intended to be played by 10-year-olds.

The other parents had not been aware of what was on this game, as one had bought it with birthday money stating 'all of his friends played it', so they assumed it was fine. They were shocked, confiscated the game and addressed the content with their son. The tone of their conversations with Laura had been threatening and frightening for her. She had become anxious about boys and being around boys, believing they were going to hurt and kill her. This had a very real impact on her emotional well-being. Because she spoke about the incidents quickly and her parents referred her quickly, we were able to ensure she recovered well from the experience and emerged from the process with new thinking and fresh perspective on the incident. Please ensure you play the games you are giving your children ahead of handing them over or at the very least that you sit in and observe them playing it the first time... and adhere to the age restrictions on these games.

The content of some of these games can lead a child to search for related content online and as a result it is not that unusual for a child aged 8–12 years to view online pornography. One of the main problems with children viewing online pornography at this age is that they still lack the framework of what an intimate relationship looks and feels like within which they can position and ultimately distinguish between porn-sex and what is a respectful and mutually agreeable intimate relationship. I will be discussing this topic in much more detail in book three when we look at adolescence but I mention it here because it is a topic that might come up at this stage of development.

As always, keep the lines of communication open and stay calm and curious when and if this arises. From the outset, state that you know that they might see some things online that they know they shouldn't be looking at; perhaps a friend will show them photos or videos that are for adults. Ensure that they know that they won't be in trouble for talking to you about this and that part of your job as their parent is to keep an eye on what they might see to make sure it is not the wrong stuff. If this does come up and you find yourself having to explain porn to your pre-teen, stay calm and factual. Say something like, 'It is for adults and not for children. It is acting and not real.' Emphasise that real relationships do not look like this. End with a statement about how proud you are that they could talk to you about this and remind them that if anyone tries to show them stuff like this they should turn away, and if they see it by accident or someone sends it to them while playing online they should come straight to you about it and you will deal with it. Remind them that they are never in trouble for telling the truth. This is a *no shame, no blame* approach that keeps the lines of communication open and allows you to grow this conversation and its content up as your child grows up. They need to know that the cringey conversations are welcome and invited too.

Video gaming can have both a pro-social and an anti-social impact on users. Moderating content and access time and ensuring that you are a part of this online gaming world with them and aware of what they are doing will go a long way to directing it more towards the pro-social end of things. The anti-social is that it can over-stimulate some children and cause them to become aggressive, both physically and in thoughts and feelings. If your child has a tendency to become over-stimulated and hyper-aroused, be aware that they will likely need and benefit from regular breaks in their usage and will need a countdown so that their time doesn't abruptly end (in other words, the end happens with them not to them). You can use something like a 15-minute sand timer and say that when the sand hits the bottom they must log off from what they are doing. Agreeing a usage contract/set of rules in advance of them getting the console/device is also very useful; involve them in designing this and agreeing the timings and stick it up on a wall to refer back to. Regardless of how it affects them, try to do

15 minutes of interactive play when they come off to ensure that you reorient them to the real rather than virtual world.

15-minute play

Consider challenge play with added nurture built in – do three rounds of thumb wrestling. Curling your hands together so that you make one fist-like grip between you, lie your thumbs flat side by side then move your thumbs side to side saying *1, 2, 3, 4, I declare a thumb war, 5, 6, 7, 8,* try to keep your thumb straight (you set the pace and don't let them speed you up). The object is that one of you holds the other's thumb down for a count of three. Repeat it with your other hands and then you cross your arms and do two thumbs together. Increase the structure here by placing your hands on a cushion and saying your hands have to stay on the cushion – this will be more grounding and regulating for a hyper-aroused child. Once you have done three rounds (the child really should win two out of three rounds), say that you want to make it a bit harder this time and cover your hands with lotion and then cover their hands with lotion. Rub it in for them saying you want to make sure that their hands are really slippy up to the tips of their fingers (this is the nurture piece as it is like a hand massage without calling it that). Now repeat three rounds as above but the tactile transfer of the lotion makes it more challenging to grip while also making it a more sensory engaged activity.

DEATH, DYING AND SERIOUS ILLNESS

By the age of four years old, many children can grasp the finality of death. Between four and six years old, children become quite fascinated with themes of death and dying, even if no one close to them is sick or has died. It is good to speak openly about death and to use clear, unambiguous language. Avoiding phrases like 'someone has passed away', 'is no longer with us', 'we have lost them' and instead choosing to say that someone we love and care about has died and won't be coming back is much more helpful for young children.

Becky (five years old) was referred to see me following the death of her beloved grandfather who had been ill for some time. Her parents worried she wasn't accepting his death and kept asking for him and if they knew where he was. They felt they had prepared her well by talking openly about him being very sick and too sick to get better. It didn't take long to get to the crux of Becky's struggle as she was barely in the room with me when she turned and indignantly said, 'Well, are YOU going to help find Granddad for me?'

I was confused and wondered how she thought I would do that.

She said, 'Mum and Dad keep telling people that we've lost Granddad but no one is looking for him and I'm so sad that he must be scared on his own. We have to find him and bring him home.'

Becky had not understood that Granddad was dead. I suggested I have a quick chat with Mum and Dad and that we would all sit together and clear this up.

Sitting down and telling Becky clearly, 'We weren't very clear about what we said. Granddad isn't lost, he's dead. The doctors tried really hard to make him better but it was a tricky sickness and he died,' she exclaimed, 'Oh no, that's so sad, I wish he wasn't dead, I wish I could see and talk to him.'

She understood that dead meant he wasn't coming back and she could start to grieve for him in her own way. How we say it is very important, and often the language is tricky for us so we dilute it to make it easier to say rather than to hear. Children need clear, unambiguous language to fully integrate the message.

Between the ages of six and nine years old, children show a clearer understanding of death with increased focus on the physical and biological aspects of illness and death, including asking questions such as 'What happens to your body after you die?', 'What happens to the body when it's in the ground?' and 'Do doctors cut people open after they die to take a look inside or take their organs out?' However, there is still evidence of magical and omnipotent thinking present and they may believe that they can even wish death on someone ('I hate you, I wish you were dead') or wish them back to life ('I asked God to send my nanny back to us and he didn't listen' or 'I'm asking Santa to bring Daddy back to us this Christmas').

By about nine years old their concept of death is similar to that of an adult and they grasp that death is not reversible or transient *but* still believe it is something that happens to *others* and not to them or their family. They may also still personify death, seeing death as a character that can be drawn or visualised.

From nine to 12 years old this awareness continues to mature and develop and they grasp that death can happen to them and their loved ones. The biological curiosity intensifies with questions about stiffness and temperature and colour of a body emerging. With this increased awareness of death and its finality comes increased anxiousness that it will affect them and their lives. We often hear about an interest in what happens after death, not only to the dead person but also to those left behind, including the child themselves. One of the mistakes we as parents make is that after someone special dies and our children wonder what will happen to them if *we* were to die, we tend to dismiss their fears with a statement like 'Oh don't worry, I'm not going to die.'

Amy (ten years old) was referred to see me following the sudden and unexpected death of her father. Her mother was worried that she wasn't coping at all well with this loss and six months after he had died was still following her around the house and refusing to leave her side. She was developing what her mother understood as separation anxiety. I wasn't so sure this explained what she was experiencing and agreed to meet with her. Amy was very quiet and withdrawn; she avoided eye contact with me and only responded to direct questions and did so in a low voice. I orientated her to my therapy space and to the sand tray and the clay and art materials. I sensed that this means of expression would appeal to her.

We spent a number of weeks communicating in this non-verbal way. She completed a number of sand-tray activities and it was while we were moulding some clay, about six sessions into our work, that she looked up at me and said, 'But what will happen to me and my brother and sister if my mum dies too?'

I reflected that it was a good and important question and repeated it back to her, emphasising, 'Well, Amy, you tell me – what would happen to you guys?'

She didn't know and this was the cause of huge anxiety inside her. She spoke about how she knew that she could take care of her younger siblings for two weeks based on there being food in the house and an emergency money jar in the kitchen. This money would allow her to buy the bread and milk they'd need for two weeks given that the local shop was on the same side of the road as their house so she could take the younger two with her without dealing with getting them across a busy road.

I exhaled loudly and sat back in my chair. 'Wow, Amy! You've really thought this through and you have a great plan in mind, but I'm hearing that you don't see yourself being able to manage for much more than two weeks. I think we need to bring your mum in and make a longer-term plan together.'

I met and spoke with her mum first and she said that Amy had been asking her since her dad died about what would happen to them if she were to die too, but she had wanted to make her feel better so kept saying, 'Oh I'm not going to die, it's okay.' Amy reflected to her mum that her dad used to say that too… and then he died.

We sat down and made a plan as to where she and her siblings would go to live and who with and how this would change depending on how old they all were if and when Mum died. Mum also told Amy that she takes good care of her health and has regular check-ups with the doctor to do her best to stay healthy (this really mattered to Amy as her dad had died of a sudden heart attack). Knowing there was a plan in place alleviated much of Amy's anxiety and she was able to let her mum go about her day and found it easier to separate to go to school, and this continued to improve steadily over time.

This type of egocentrism of death is developmentally normal and will actually increase as they move into adolescence when they will see themselves as immortal and begin to romanticise death (as they tend to see reflected back in much of teen drama, TV, movies and even books). We will look at this piece in more detail in book three but as some parents will see glimpses of this behaviour pattern emerging in their pre-teens I wanted to include a mention of it here too. This is also the age where the questions and musings about the meaning of life, what it is all about, what the point is of life and all the day-to-day mundanities if we all die in the end anyway begin to arise. These questions are not for you to answer but you can enter into a reflective state with your pre-teen about them instead ('Sometimes I wonder this. What do you come up with as answers?') and try to share a moment of meeting as they philosophise life and death. This is developmentally normal and even healthy – even if it feels as if they are doing it to test you!

Play with this – yes really!

This is about being *playful* in terms of how you offer opportunity to process difficult things. For your 15-minute play with your children about death and dying start by getting into the head space of your child developmentally; what is their understanding and the belief system of your family around death? Some of you will have heaven/an afterlife and so on, and some of you will not and will advocate that death is the end. There is no right or wrong on this but be consistent within your narrative. The playfulness comes from being open and inviting in terms of how you approach this. Consider role-playing conversations or imagine a phone call with the person. What would you like to say and what might they say back (keep it positive in responses)? You could sit and write a letter together to the person – you might even take this to a postbox and 'post' it to the person wherever you locate them as now being (mostly useful if you have heaven or an afterlife in your belief system). Being *playful* is a state of being, it is a state of mind and it certainly doesn't have to be focused on making light or fun of a serious loss. It is about staying connected and engaged in how you invite the processing of that loss. That is what I mean when I say *play with this*.

Memory boards: When someone special dies, a nice way to remember them and what you shared together is to make a memory board. You will need a cork board, some board pins and a range of photos (scissors to cut and glue to stick) and things like ticket stubs (from entry to movies or fun parks, etc.) or favourite sweet/chocolate wrappers, or you could press a favourite flower and then place it in some laminate paper. Arrange all on the board and talk and share memories of the person and the events as you do so. You can hang the board somewhere everyone can see initially and, perhaps, over time move it to hang on the inside of a closet door so it can be looked at whenever needed rather than all the time.

Balloon messaging: Write a message, draw a picture or a symbol (such as a heart) on a piece of paper that you then roll up and push inside a balloon before blowing it up and tying the top. Now take it outside on a windy day or in a windy place (or use helium) and let it go. This is a symbolic letting go as well and gives an opportunity to say whatever last words your child doesn't feel that they got to say.

Make a legacy box/poster: This is best for the older end of this age group. As they think about death and question what the meaning of life is, sit and decide what legacy message they would like to leave behind. Start by saying, 'Imagine you are very old, say 106 years old, and you are dying – what would you want to have achieved/done/visited/who would be in your family/how would you want them to think of you/what adventures would you have had...' and so on, and turn all of this into a poster or smaller memorabilia that can go into a box. Talk about obituaries and read a few together. Take turns writing each other's or your own, always from the perspective of being VERY old at the end of a long and lived life.

Practice death on plants and animals: This is useful for younger children too. Have them plant seeds that they are responsible for growing and taking care of. Don't worry if they over- or under-water because there is a lesson in either outcome that is important to learn for themselves. When you see plants or flowers that have died, say so: 'Oh, these flowers are dead, let's add them to the compost so they can break down and decompose now.' Even when your children are very young, talk about insects and plants that die and use that language. If you have family pets, losing one can be as close to losing a person (perhaps not all pets – goldfish tend to have a shorter life span but when it is a dog or cat it can be a very deep relationship). Losing a pet is often a child's first experience with death and grief and as such ensure that you afford it the space and respect it deserves. Use correct language and have a ceremony to mark the pet's death, do a memory collage/ photo together and talk about your pet and how much fun and love you shared. This is a good way to introduce the stages of grief and the process of death, funerals and burials to children.

BREAKING THE NEWS OF A PARENTAL BREAK-UP

The end of a relationship is a difficult choice and experience for the adults involved, never mind the children. And just like the air stewards advise us on aeroplanes, you must attend to your own air mask before attending to theirs. What I mean by this is give yourself adequate time to process the decision to separate and to come together on a shared narrative and plan for how your children will be co-parented by you before you sit down with them. If this cannot be the case and the separation is more abrupt or perhaps the details cannot be agreed on in a timely way, then you will need to sit with your children and tell them that one of you is moving out and what this means for them. Emphasise that the grown-ups are still working out all of the details and you will keep them updated on this as there will be some of their questions you will not be able to answer if the split is sudden, acrimonious or subject to ongoing court hearings regarding custody and access arrangements. My rule of thumb is that you should always be honest but developmentally appropriate with children, even and perhaps especially when it comes to these more life-changing events. And parents separating is a life-changing event, even when you manage it really well for all involved.

The details of your separation will be particular to your given situation but the truth is that, as much as we may try, we will not be able to fully shield or protect our children from what is happening and perhaps we shouldn't try so hard to do that. Our children are members of our family unit and when that unit is coming apart they should be privy (in developmentally appropriate ways) to what is happening so that the change happens *with* rather than *to* them.

If your children are close in age developmentally and it is possible for you both to sit with them for a conversation, do so. If your children need to hear the information in different ways, sit with and tell them individually. As best you can, try to manage the dynamic so that both parents can be present for this conversation.

It might go something like this: 'We have made a difficult choice to end our marriage/relationship and won't be living together anymore. Mum/Dad will be moving out of the house and will be living somewhere else. Our relationship changed and while we are no longer in love with each other, we both really love you and always will. We are still your parents and will always work together as parents for you, but we feel that we can do the best job we can as friends rather than being in a relationship together.'

Depending on the situation, maybe there has been a lot of rowing in your home, or unpleasant tensions (and again with a child at this stage of development it would be naïve to think they haven't picked up on some of that), you might add in, 'As you know, we haven't been getting along and there have been more rows and arguments in our home recently. That's not what any of us want and it isn't good for any of us.'

While there may well be more details pertaining to your separation, be that an affair or one of you is leaving to go straight into a new relationship, your children do not (yet) need to know about this. Steps should be taken to be discreet and be mindful that it is enough for young children to process that their parents are separating before they learn any more details like these.

Children of this age (and younger) are still quite egocentric so the main question for them is: 'How will this affect me and my life?' This is perfectly normal and understandable and you should plan to address this before they have to ask it. You might say something like, 'You're going to keep living in this home as you always have with X parent and you'll be staying with X parent in X location on X days/weekends. You'll be going to your same school with your same friends and most things really will stay the same for you, but the stuff that's changing is also big stuff so we want you to know that you can ask us any questions you have, now or as we move forward.'

This is, of course, if they will be staying in their family home and local school. If the home needs to be sold as part of the separation, speak about the present, not offering any future guarantees: 'For now, you'll stay living with Mum/Dad in our home. We're working out what will work best for all of us in the future, but if anything is to change we'll tell you about it. For now X, Y, Z stays the same though.'

Be mindful that if your home needs to be sold you do tell your children directly so that they don't hear it elsewhere. Be clear that a decision has been made by the adults and that it is not open for negotiation *but* accept and empathise with their emotional response to this decision: 'I understand that you're angry and upset that we have to move out of our home. Change is really hard, especially when it isn't a change you got to choose. We tried to look at all of the options and we agreed that this is the only way we can all be taken care of. So we're moving to X (do try to have a plan in place before sharing the news if possible) and you'll get to decorate a new bedroom, we'll be close to X amenity (football grounds, park, aquarium, zoo, forest) so you'll like that. We're also a bit nervous about this new change so we do get it, but we'll help each other through it.' Bear in mind that it is okay if they tantrum, strop out of the room, shout and cry. Give them space to react and then be available for comfort and repair afterwards.

To be this emotionally available to your children in what is bound to be a very difficult time for you, you will need to activate your own support network of friends and family around you. You do not need (well-meaning) people who are there to tell you what to do or how to feel because you already know this yourself. You do, however, need people who will hold you up, support you and pour the requisite tea/wine/beers and just listen and accept where you are at. Get out for walks to just breathe and ground yourself. Importantly though, do have a person you can be yourself with, someone you can let rip at and say all of the emotive things you try so hard to conceal from your ex-partner and your children for the greater good, someone who will accept and hold that for and with you so that you can stay connected with the bigger process.

Modelling good self-care is important for your children, and if you do fall apart and cry or lose it in front of them, do not beat yourself up – you are human and this is a very difficult experience for anyone to go through.

Once you have calmed and settled, go to your child and acknowledge what has happened: 'I really fell apart there for a while. I guess everything just got a bit much and my feelings exploded. This is hard for me too, but I want you to know that it will all get easier, and I'm now feeling calm and okay. Sometimes it's good to let ourselves fall apart a bit, isn't it? You should know that if that happens to you, I'll help put you back together every time.'

STRUGGLING WITH THE STRUGGLE TO FIT IN

I've spoken about friendships already but this particular aspect is often the trickiest conversation because it can be excruciating to watch our children struggle to fit in. The temptation to jump in and rescue them from that struggle and manage the friendship or play experience so that they can seemingly 'fit in' is very real and very understandable and yet… don't do it! Yes, I am saying leave them to struggle – mild to moderately, but never let it cross into bullying or targeted isolation (although for most children it is a struggle and nothing more sinister than that).

Why on earth would I advise you to leave your 8–12-year-old child to struggle? I am not saying this in a sadistic or cruel way – as I hope you have gleaned by now, I always advocate kindness and compassion in parenting – but the kindest thing here is to step back (not step away entirely just step back) so that they can feel and think and work their way through the struggle. It is in the struggle to fit in that they will learn the all-important social skills to handle challenging social situations, to negotiate boundaries with new groups of people and peers, to work out who they do fit with and to empathise with how it feels to be left out or be on the outside of friendship groups. There is so much learning in this struggle that you would be doing your child a disservice by jumping in prematurely and 'fixing' it for them.

So what can you do to support them in this struggle? Well, be available for them to come to you to work through the struggle and associated feelings they have with it. Keep that all-important door of parent–child communication open and be available with lots of **reflective listening skills** and empathy. Talk about what they could do now to change the situation and even or especially when you don't think their suggestion will effect the type of change they desire, say something like, 'Well done, it sounds as if you've really thought about this and have come up with an idea. We can talk about how that goes afterwards if you like.'

As parents, we tend to assume that we are truly listening to our children when they talk to us, but from conversations I have with children of this age, they say that we listen to what they say while thinking of what we will say back. This results in us hearing *what* is said but missing non-verbal cues as to *how* it is said. Take a few minutes now (and repeat as and when you need to as this should not be a one-off exercise) and take this effective listening quiz.

EFFECTIVE LISTENING QUIZ

READ THE FOLLOWING QUESTIONS AND CIRCLE THE ANSWER THAT MOST APPLIES TO YOU AT THIS POINT IN TIME. YOU CAN REVISIT THIS QUIZ TIME AND AGAIN AS YOU REQUIRE IT

Question 1: When your child is talking to you, do you stop what you are doing?

Yes
No
Sometimes
I don't know

Question 2: Do you give your child your full attention when they are talking?

Yes
No
Sometimes
I don't know

Question 3: Do you interrupt when your child is speaking?

Yes
No
Sometimes
I don't know

Question 4: Do you repeat what you think you heard your child say, just to be clear?

Yes

No

Sometimes

I don't know

Question 5: When your child is asking you about a problem, are you already thinking of the solution before they are done speaking?

Yes

No

Sometimes

I don't know

Question 6: Do you fold your arms in front of you when are upset by listening to your child's explanations?

Yes

No

Sometimes

I don't know

Question 7: Do you look at your child when they are speaking to you?

Yes

No

Sometimes

I don't know

Question 8: Do you ask questions to keep the conversation going or when you don't understand something your child is saying?

Yes

No

Sometimes

I don't know

Question 9: Do you offer other ways for your child to 'talk' to you, like social networking, texting and email?

Yes

No

Sometimes

I don't know

Question 10: Do you encourage your child to talk again later by telling them you are there to listen if they need you or by 'wondering' how the thing you spoke about is now?

Yes

No

Sometimes

I don't know

Now take some time to reflect on how your answers have made you feel. What learning is there in this?

Active listening is, without doubt, one of the most beneficial and effective parenting tools you can have. It is a way of listening to someone that conveys in a 'doing' way that you are present and with them, that you hear and understand their perspective (this doesn't mean agreeing necessarily) and have gained a deeper awareness and appreciation of the situation or event they are describing. Active listening is about accepting, not teaching. We may know that some of what our child is telling us is untrue or at least a generalisation but what matters in the moment is that they feel their emotional experience is understood and validated by you.

Sam and his dad came to see me. Sam, aged nine, was very upset at the start of our session so Dad sat down beside him and began to tell me what was up with Sam. I suggested we let Sam do that instead.

Sam opened with, 'Everyone in my class is invited to X's birthday party except me.'

Dad interjected straight away with a clarification: 'Well, it's not everyone, Sam, because I know that David isn't invited either.'

Sam exploded at Dad, shouting at him that he didn't know anything about it and that David isn't even going to be around on the day and added, 'Before you say anyone else's name who isn't coming, it's a sports party and not everyone is good at sports.'

I cued Dad that I would step in on this. I sighed loudly and said, 'Sam, you're really disappointed that you haven't been included in this party. It makes you angry to think that only the kids who are good at sports get to go when you really like sports too.'

Dad got it quickly and said to Sam, 'I'm sorry that I didn't pay attention to how this felt for you. What would make it feel a bit better for you?'

Sam was dismissive and a little closed off initially so I suggested we hold that thought and start some play for now. I moved into challenge play that had Sam and Dad work collaboratively against me. By making them a team and having them work together on the same side we were working through any residual tension from Dad's misstep (as Sam experienced it). By keeping some competitive element in the play, I was supporting him in working through some of the edge that his frustration had left in him.

At the end of his session, I reflected how well Sam and Dad worked as a team, and as they were putting on their coats he said to Dad, 'Maybe we could go to the adventure centre on Saturday (day of the party) and do some rock climbing on their climbing wall?'

Dad said, 'What a great idea; thanks for inviting me. I would love to do that with you.'

Had Dad simply offered to take him out to do something else on the day of the party while Sam was still 'in' his heightened emotional arousal about feeling excluded, Sam would most likely have rejected the offer. But by waiting, validating his feelings about the experience and allowing him to process those feelings by 'doing' not saying, Dad enabled him to come up with a solution himself. Dad may well have been right about plenty of other kids not being invited either but by using logic and reasoning he inadvertently dismissed Sam's emotional experience in an attempt to make him feel better.

When we make ourselves truly available to listen, when we stop what we are doing and give our child our full and undivided attention, we are letting them know that they are worthy and deserving of our attention and focus. We are communicating that they, and their issue, are our priority in that moment.

In reflecting back not only what we have heard but how we have heard it, including references to how we have understood them to be feeling about the matter, we are letting them know that we have heard their struggle and distress and that we believe that their view of the world/the issue at hand is a valid one from their perspective.

By stepping back and wondering what they think they should do to bring about an outcome/change in the situation, we are letting them know that we trust them to know what to do. We are empowering them to take a chance on their own solution and to practise independence. They might be successful or they might fail in this attempt, but they will learn from it either way, and it is through repeated experiences like this that they grow and develop in their social and problem-solving skills.

It takes lots and lots of practice to get this right, so give yourself a break. Bear in mind that you want to listen with acceptance and not judgement. You are accepting how your child is feeling and not judging the facts of what they are saying or if you believe their feeling to be in or out of proportion. By tuning into how your child is feeling, you will bring them deeper into how they are feeling about it and allow them to feel felt and that you 'get' them. By staying outside the situation yourself – so not what *you* would do but staying with your child as they work out what *they* can do – you show that any and all feelings your child has are equally acceptable to you.

Practice

Take this (very common) example now: *Your child declares that they hate school, they are not going to go anymore because it is boring and they don't learn anything there anyway.*

Now I invite you to write out what you will say in response to this using *acceptance*, staying out of *judgement*, *reflecting what* you have heard and *how* your child sounds saying it and *wondering* how they will work their way through the struggle or *manage the struggle* they are in.

When you have written yourself a short script, **practise** saying it aloud. Ideally say it to someone who can respond for you or record yourself saying it aloud and listen back afterwards, reflecting on how it might feel to have someone respond to you in this way. You can tweak and amend as you feel you need to, based on this.

I might say something like, 'That's awful that you're finding school so boring because you're very clever and deserve to be challenged and engaged in school.' Maybe this elicits some more information in response – *'Yeah and it's not like the teacher can do anything about it because all of his time is spent on getting these kids to listen.'*

Now you can add in, 'It really bothers you that all of the class time is taken up on a small group of kids' behaviour and you're not learning anything new. That must be really frustrating for you.'

The child might reply, *'That's why I don't want to go anymore – there's no point; it's always the same,'* and you can say, 'Oh I understand, it's not just the other kids you're frustrated with, it's also with the teacher for not getting it sorted. You want him to be able to change the situation so that you can get what you need out of class time too.'

This may elicit something like, *'Yes, exactly, I think a few of us should get together and talk to the teacher after classes end tomorrow.'*

This is not intended to read as a script for you but more like a template to guide you through a potentially fractious conversation that could go from: 'I don't want to go to school because it's boring' to you snapping, 'Well tough luck, you have to go to school so get on with it.' At no point in the above have I said *you must go to school* but by the end I have brought the conversation to a place whereby the young person has said they are going into school so they can address the problem.

You can use your knowledge of your child to intuit how they might be feeling about a situation and to read their body language and tone of voice. Subtly mirror back some of their non-verbal cues to them, as this reinforces that you are understanding them (in a *feeling* way) and what they are thinking and feeling. Subtlety is the key. You are not mirroring everything they do but you might gradually move your hand to your hip if they are or slouch to the side they are, and aim to match the essence of their tone of voice (that is not mimicking, which would feel as if you are making fun of them).

Make sure you have the time to do this and hold in mind that most feelings are transitory and will pass. Allow your child to draw their own conclusions and remember that just because a solution didn't emerge doesn't mean that your active listening didn't work. Our goal here is not to 'fix' the child or situation but for your child to feel heard and understood and for you to use this communication method to deepen your relationship with your child at this crucial stage of development.

Do not use this approach if your child needs specific information from you or is not in the mood to talk at all (simply say that you are available to listen whenever they feel ready) or if reassurance, encouragement or correction are what is called for. Perhaps you are too low or empty yourself. You may be exhausted and be juggling too much to be able to sit and offer gentle active listening about school when all you need is for them to get into the car so you can all leave the house. Be honest with yourself and your child: 'I'd love to be able to give this time now but I really can't. I'll come back to you this evening at 7 p.m. when other stuff is done and we can really think and talk about it together because it's important that I can give you my full attention and I can't do that right now.' You attend to these first and then you might use your active listening when the situation is calmer or more open.

This is to show you what you can do to support your child through a struggle rather than jump in and pull them out while you mop the struggle up beneath them. This kind of parenting response is no less active but it is far more effective at bringing about long-term meaningful change for your child and strengthening your relationship.

---

15 minutes of play to stay or reconnect

Play tip: These activities promote co-regulation and connection, which is important after a difficult conversation. Play will help to take us out of our cognitive and thinking brain space into our emotional and feeling brain space and come out of our heads and into the 'now' moment of being together.

Jelly/Ice cream: Every time you say 'jelly' your child should say 'ice cream' but they should say it the same way that you do. This means if you yell JELLY they yell ICE CREAM or if you whisper *jelly* they whisper *ice cream*. And so on. Get creative using funny voice sounds or pick two foods that they like or perhaps use your family favourites to personalise this a little more for them.

Eye signals: Start with having the child lead, which affords them more control at a time when they might need to assert themselves and their sense of authority but does so within your parental boundaries and structure of the activity. Say you will follow their cues for 10 moves and then they will be your mirror for five moves. The person leading keeps their head perfectly straight and only their eyes move. The person observing must move in accordance with the direction of the eye movements (if sitting they should wave the hand to the side the eyes move to, but if standing up then they can jump to the side being gestured to). If eyes look to the wall, you wave or jump towards that wall or window (left/right in other words) and if eyes look up to the ceiling you either wave hands above head or jump forwards, and a look down towards the floor warrants a low wave or a jump backwards. If they roll or blink their eyes, you either roll your hands in front of you or turn around if standing.

DE-MYSTIFYING THE MYTH YET KEEPING MAGIC ALIVE

Middle childhood is also the stage of development when many childhood beliefs are shed and pushed aside. This can be a challenging experience for children and parents alike.

Most children won't get too far into middle childhood without at least learning of rumours about the existence of Santa, the Easter Bunny, the Tooth Fairy and so on, and will either work it out for themselves or turn to their parents for 'the truth'. It can be very tempting to protect their innocence and maintain the beautiful myth, but by the time they are asking you they are ready for some kind of answer.

The safest approach is to start with reflecting their question back to them: 'Well, since you're asking me about this, I wonder what your own belief about this is?'

I like to share this truth: 'So long as you believe, I mean truly believe, then Santa/the Easter Bunny/the Tooth Fairy are real and very much in your life. But when you stop believing and in your heart you feel it differently, then they stop being real for you and you're quite right, that is when mums and dads take over those roles for you.'

Letting go of beliefs is sad and difficult, and there can be a type of grieving associated with it. Let them know you are sad this time is now over *but* that surprises will continue to be a part of their life and you will still enjoy doing this for them. If there are younger children, ensure that you secure their commitment that they will uphold the belief for their younger siblings, and perhaps involve them in the gift buying for the others too.

Learning the truth doesn't and shouldn't spell an end to magical tradition and rituals. Continue to celebrate the process by making a big deal of decorating the house/tree and sharing stories. Develop a family tradition that you know will stand the test of time regardless of age.

I like to do this one. On Christmas Eve, exchange a book and a bar of each person's favourite chocolate once everyone is in their new Christmas pyjamas. Everyone takes their book and chocolate to bed nice and early in preparation for the special day ahead. This one can continue long into adulthood; in fact, you will find that these traditions grow to mean even more as children grow up – so says the grown woman who still receives a Christmas stocking from Santa in her parents' house each year!

TOP 10 TIPS WHEN HAVING DIFFICULT CONVERSATIONS!

1. Use your active listening skills and watch out for those door slammers.
2. Talk often with your child to bring out positive opinions, ideas and behaviours by using an affirmative tone and body language. Don't just wait for the difficult conversations but invest in open communication often and early.
3. Treat your child with the same respect you would have them treat you. Say 'Hi', 'I love you', 'How was your day? and so on. Also ensure you always use 'please' and 'thank you' even when you are correcting their behaviour, for example, 'Please shut my car door gently next time.'

4. Remember that your tone of voice is extremely important. Yelling simply doesn't work. The loud noise will shut down the listener (your child) and you will not get through. If you feel the need to yell, take some 'time out' of the conversation until you have better control.

5. Plan ahead. Think through your main talking points and key messages you wish to convey in the conversation. Stick to those and if the conversation is being redirected by your child outside those parameters, acknowledge what is happening: 'You're bringing up some important points I hadn't thought about' or 'That is also a really important topic and we can discuss it another day but now we're talking about X.' Buy yourself time to gather your thoughts if need be: 'I'm going to need some time to think about your points and I'll come back to you on it. Thank you for helping me to think more about this.'

6. Be precise and detailed about what you expect and have agreed from the discussion. Write it down and use an action plan if you feel there is a need, but use positive language in doing so – i.e. what you want them to do as opposed to what you don't want them to do. This can go on a page to be pinned up in their room or you can start a 'Don't sweat the tricky stuff' notebook in which you summarise the messages of each difficult conversation using positive language.

7. Discuss some things together on a one-to-one basis and some things with the whole family. It is healthy to invite a variety of thoughts and ideas on subjects and this can be a fun and less intense way of approaching some of the difficult conversations. Good times often bring about great conversations and wonderful memories.

8. 'Do as I say, not as I do' doesn't work. Modelling is the best way of learning. You are your child's model and they will emulate your behaviours.

9. Never shut your child out to show that you disapprove of their behaviour, statements or beliefs. If you need time before you can talk to them about something that has upset you, tell them that you need time. Don't walk away silent.

10. Be clear that difficult conversations are not a one-way system in your family and that your child can raise a difficult topic with you too. In fact, you should encourage this. Practise with things that are in the news or pertinent to civil society as it is not so much about them as about their thoughts and beliefs on a subject. You are laying groundwork for how you all think and talk about the tricky topics so when you do want to initiate something in a more direct and focused way, it is not an unusual or awkward thing for any of you.

15-minute tip

You and your children will at some point experience at least some of the difficult discussions I've listed above, but it is just as likely that you and your child (even your individual children within your family) will come up with topics of your own. Have some fun with this by saying to your child in middle childhood (and continue this into and through the teen years) that there is a postbox in which each of you can post a tricky topic to talk about and you will take turns pulling one out each evening to spend 15 minutes talking about together. Some topics will take longer and some will need to be paused so you can find out some information and that's okay too, as you can carry them over to the next day to finish off.

Postbox: Take an old shoebox and cut a postbox style slot into the lid before you tape the lid onto the box. Now cover with nice paper or paint the box, leaving the post slot exposed. Leave it somewhere accessible and either of you can drop a general topic in that you feel needs to be talked about some more.

(**Note:** This doesn't mean something urgent or pressing should go in here and wait to be selected. Some topics need to be dealt with straight away and some will need to be talked about in general. You could have an emergency drop envelope taped to the side of the box and check that for topics first.)

CHAPTER 5

Homework vs the Great Outdoors

THE LEARNING CURVE OF HOMEWORK

To be upfront, I don't advocate homework, especially not for primary-school children. I mean, who wants to do a day's work and then come home and do more work? I don't, and you can be guaranteed your young and middle -childhood child doesn't. I hear about homework in my work all the time and it can become a hotbed for parent–child tensions.

My objections to homework include the following:

- Children need time, space and opportunity to play – this is precisely *how* they learn rather than being a break from learning.
- Sitting doing homework is a sedentary activity at a time when children need movement and physical activity.
- For some children, a busy home is not a relaxed learning environment in the way a managed classroom is, so doing this work at home is stressful.
- As they have already been 'at work' for most of their day, it should not follow them home.
- It blocks their natural creativity and innate curiosity to get out and explore their environment.

- There are no consistent reliable studies to show that homework helps school performance in any way.

Marvellous, Joanna, I hear you say, but what if we *have* to do it? Well then use playful ways to create boundaries around it and make it more fun to do. Using a 15-minute sand timer, say that your child must sit and do homework until all the sand hits the bottom. Then they get another turn of the timer to play, read a book, eat a snack or whatever. Then they must return and do one more turn of the timer to finish homework. And honestly, 30 (focused and dedicated) minutes on homework should be enough to complete it and, if not, simply write a note to the teacher stating that they spent 30 minutes on their homework doing as much of it as they could. This may well spark a face-to-face conversation with your teacher and you can and should discuss it then. The sand timer serves as a boundary for the homework and also allows them to take a break in the middle so they know they only have to do it for short bursts.

If they do homework, let it be their work and not yours. You can check over it to ensure they did all they were asked (or see/excuse what didn't get done in the time frame you gave it) but try not to correct their homework for them. If you see answers that are wrong you might ask between the first and second 15 minutes if they would like to take time to check their answers at the end. Encourage them to slow down as their handwriting is not clear enough for the teacher to read, but this is not a battle I suggest you take on as a parent. If their answers are wrong because they do not understand the material then it is important that their teacher sees this in their homework and can follow up to ensure they do understand – this comes back to what I have said earlier about not rescuing them from every struggle because there is often so much valuable growth and development to be had within that struggle.

By taking this approach to homework you can maximise some benefits from it for your child at this stage of development. These benefits include:

- the discipline of sticking with something even when you don't want to do it
- the beginning of some time-management skills
- working on increased tolerance to better manage frustration levels
- giving you some further insight into how they are coping with schoolwork and also how stress and frustration impact on their behaviour
- an opportunity to learn (perhaps better for some children) in a more comfortable and relaxed environment.

In lieu of prescribed school-curriculum homework I would happily support outdoor play (regardless of weather) as homework or being tasked to pick up three to five pieces of rubbish to properly dispose of on the way home, or encouraging parent–child and/or family play time as a homework activity.

OUTDOOR PLAY – NECESSITY NOT NOVELTY

Spending much of their day in school in a building with walls, it is really important and beneficial that children get to spend as much time as possible outdoors. It is good for physical and emotional health, encourages exploration and creativity as well as supporting motor-skills development. Time spent playing outdoors *has* been shown to improve school performance and engagement, hence all the more reason to prescribe it as homework if you are setting homework.

The great outdoors provides a space with far fewer physical restrictions than indoor environments and this allows children to express themselves more openly. Countless studies show that regular time spent playing outdoors reduces anxiety, hyperactivity, boosts mood, builds collaborative play skills and teamwork and lowers cortisol levels. When children are happier, more relaxed, more alert and attuned, they are more open to learning.

You probably know yourself the benefits to be had from a walk in fresh air to clear your head and relieve tensions – well it stands to reason that our children who are experiencing increasingly sedentary lifestyles with screens and urban noises and other such stimuli will also benefit greatly from time outdoors in nature, running, jumping and climbing.

In 2016 it was widely reported in newspaper articles that Nicky Butt, ex-footballer and the then head of the Manchester United Youth Academy was hiring circus performers to come in to work with their players to increase mobility and teach them how to fall and roll safely to avoid injury. I thought at the time (and still do now) how fascinating this is. The potential impact on motor-skills development, physical and mental health is huge and worth investing in a resource that is (largely) freely available outside our doors.

15 MINUTES OF PLAY THAT BRING IT BACK TO NATURE

Garden patch: Assign a small patch of your garden to your children and allow them to choose what vegetable or herb seeds they will plant and take care of to bring into your kitchen for you to incorporate into cooking with them. There is great creativity and nurturance in this type of play and it gives them a reason to go outside and check their patch each day. Don't interfere, let them lead and by all means follow and support them as and when they look for your help, but they should feel a sense of ownership of this.

Insect excavating: This is not nearly as technical as it sounds and involves identifying a stone or rock somewhere and slowly lifting/upturning it to see, examine and discuss the insect life you find underneath. Of course don't kill or otherwise interfere with the insects but use this as a way to discover and discuss them.

Build a bug hotel/Air Bee&Bee: In these times when climate change is a part of every young child's vernacular why not do something like this as a way of encouraging the insects into your garden to do their thing. Build an insect hotel or Air Bee&Bee (whatever you want to call it) but do so *with* your child not for them. Give them the list of materials to source and bring to the garden (old flower pots/branches/rolled cardboard such as inserts of toilet paper or kitchen roll/sticks/odd bits from around your garden or local park area/timber/bits of brick/bamboo. You may need to visit a garden centre with them). You can source the bigger stuff like scissors to cut bamboo. You can make a large-scale fancy-looking structure or keep it quite simple and small. The simplest way to make it is to get an old flowerpot with the bottom missing. Insert bamboo (cut to size) into the holes in the flowerpot and leave the cut ends exposed. In no time your bug hotel will have residents moving in.

I was outside my house with my own child and we spotted a very unwell-looking bumblebee barely moving and eliciting a very meek buzz. She was immediately concerned about him and how we could help. As with many small children, she felt a snack and a song would help him feel better. So we took a tablespoon and filled it with water and sugar mixed and brought it out to the little bee, placing it very close to him and gave him a small nudge towards it. She sang him a song (an adaptation of the ant song, making it the bees they buzzed one by one hurrah hurrah... up to 10). Already we could see the spoon was energizing our little bee friend and we left him alone until 20 minutes later he upped and flew away. We were thrilled and it meant I could reflect with my toddler on how nice it is to show kindness when someone needs help. This was a great way to reinforce some nurture play to build empathy skills.

More outdoor play tips and suggestions

Tag: One child is 'it'. Rounds of rock/paper/scissors should agree who is 'on' or **Eeny, meeny, miny mo, catch a tiger by the toe, if he squeals let it go, eeny meeny, miny, mo.** It is up to the child who is 'on' to chase the others and *tag* someone else to now be 'on'. And the game continues for as long as they like.

Red rover (a favourite of mine from my own school play-ground days): The children form two teams of equal numbers (ideally) and these teams stand opposite each other in lines, a decent distance apart. The first team (again use one of the above methods to decide who will go first) agrees among themselves to call one player from the other team over calling out *Red rover, Red rover, send (NAME) over.* That named person runs towards the other team's line (linked by holding hands) and attempts to charge through breaking the links. If successful, that child gets to select a player from the other team to now join their team and that team has to call someone over. If that child is unsuccessful at breaking through, they simply join the opposing team as a member, and the game continues. This is a great one for groups of kids but also family playtime outdoors.

Water play: The children run through a sprinkler or simply play with a basin of water to make wet footprints, or splash or fill a water squirter or wash some toys.

Digging for treasure: Bury something in a hole in the garden and have your child dig with their hands or a small (child's) gardening shovel to find it. It can be nice to lead from this to some water play as they can wash the mud off the item and themselves afterwards.

Patio art: Give them some chalk (pavement chalk is larger and especially good for this) and simply let them draw pictures. If some structure is needed here, set them a theme and they can draw within that theme. This can be useful if you have more than one child and they are encroaching on each other's drawings.

Hopscotch: Using your pavement chalk, draw a hopscotch game and take turns playing.

Hide and seek: This is a great outdoor game too and offers opportunity to conceal oneself and the joy of being discovered, as well as the freedom and movement of running around.

Skipping: Take a rope and if there are three or more of you take turns so that two of you hold either end of the rope while one jumps in the middle as the rope is turned. (Note: If there are two of you, tie the rope to a pole/wall/gate/tree at one end and turn the other.) *Challenge opportunity:* There is a fun way to increase the level of challenge with this game by having the person in the middle jump while holding a cup of water. Of course, the water will slosh and come out and at the end when everyone has had a turn, measure who has the most water left in his or her cup to 'win'.

Tug of war: Using your skipping rope, divide into teams (of two or more) and play with pulling the rope both ways. *Nurture opportunity:* Increase the nurture here by pulling your child into you in an embrace/group hug when you pull them over the line towards you, or let them pull you over and topple into their arms for a hug or group hug.

Limbo: Using the same rope tied to two structures (bring two chairs outside and use them) vary the heights as you and your child(ren) take turns limbo-ing under the rope to see how low each can go.

Spinning and cloud gazing: This is super simple and fun. Feel the joy of just spinning around in the garden/park area to the point of feeling dizzy and letting yourself fall over. Look up to the sky as it spins and settles then name what shape formations you can discern in the clouds in the sky while you lie side by side.

Make a thumb ball: This is a ball that you toss between you and when you catch it you read and do the action under your right thumb. You can buy thumb balls that have actions or feelings or social story prompts on them, *but* you can also make your own. Take a ball such as a blow up or foam ball (something light that won't cause injury when tossed between you). If focusing on **social skills,** write various instructions around it such as *Give the person opposite you a compliment* or *Introduce yourself to the person on your left using a funny voice* or *Make eye contact with the person on your right for five seconds* or *Shake hands with someone in the group.* Or you could **focus on actions:** *Kick a pretend ball and score imaginary goal; Swim; Hop on one leg; Play the guitar; Dance like an octopus* and so on. A more verbal version would be to share social stories using a first/best/worst option, for example you might land on something like *holiday* and you tell a story that is about your first holiday, best holiday or worst holiday. Include lots of life experiences. I love thumb balls as they are a great way to build social skills in a group setting either indoors or outdoors.

CHAPTER 6

Building Resilience and Self-Esteem

'EVERYBODY IS LOOKING AT ME' – THE EGOCENTRISM OF PRE-ADOLESCENCE

This can start to emerge slowly and gradually throughout this middle-childhood stage of development but will really come into its own around 11–12 years old. Egocentrism has two distinct elements to it:

1. Everybody else – your child believes that everyone else notices and cares (a lot) about their looks/image/behaviour.
2. Themselves – your child believes that no one else experiences things or has ever felt the feelings that they do.

This means that children in this pre-adolescent stage feel simultaneously vulnerable and invincible. Toddlerhood is the other really egocentric stage of development, and in lots of ways adolescence is a second bite at the developmental apple. However, the distinct difference is that pre-adolescents are aware that others will/may have opposing points of view to their own and toddlers are oblivious to this fact. Being aware of this just makes your pre-adolescent even more self-conscious about himself or herself, from the inside out.

You know this feeling – you lived through and emerged from this stage of development in your own pre-adolescence. Despite the fact that your child is telling you that *you don't understand, what would you know about it,* the reality is that you know quite a lot about it and, as always, knowledge is power. However, it can be very difficult to access what you know when you are in the firing line. The reason for this is that the proximity to the emotional onslaught causes you to *flip your lid.* You lose access to your thinking/reasoning brain (neo-cortex) and sink into your emotional centre (amygdala), which is firing you the fight/flight/freeze cues that make you reactive to the situation and block you from being reflective.

Self-Reflective Exercise

Reflect on your pre-adolescent self as you recall it. Ask yourself:

- What was it like to be that age? How did I feel? What did I think of myself/others/the world outside me and the people in it?
- What made me sad/mad/glad at that age? How did I show those feelings?
- How do I recall others responding to my behaviour and me at that age and how did that response make me feel at the time? How does thinking about it make me feel now?
- Now ask your parents (if that is an option available to you) or a sibling/family member how they would answer these same questions *about* you.
- Where do the answers align/diverge? What is the learning for you in this?

- Finally, reflect on *how you wish you were responded to at this stage of development and what difference might that have made to you.*

Being preoccupied with other people's perception of you, as you perceive it, is not an easy headspace to occupy. You are likely to see heightened states of emotional dysregulation as your pre-teen struggles to reconcile their changing and evolving sense of self with their (often negatively biased) sense of others' awareness. Being able to empathically connect is a very good starting point in terms of how you will support your child in managing their emotional egocentrism.

Trying to hit your own emotional pause button so that you don't get pulled into the heat of the situation with them is key. Stand firm, close your eyes, take a deep breath in and exhale slowly and deeply out. Repeat this if necessary. Then respond in a gentle yet firm tone of voice. (**When in doubt, go to A&E – Acceptance and Empathy** – but hold in mind that accepting your child's position and empathising with the feelings that drive their position does not mean you condone any overt behaviour. Acceptance and empathy are most effective within the framework of your parental boundaries and limit setting.)

I hear that you are upset and angry right now because your favourite jeans are not washed and dried for you to wear to your friend's house. (Acknowledge their feeling in a tone of acceptance.)

We don't yell at each other in this family but I get that yelling is what you feel like doing when you feel frustrated like this. (Set a limit on how they are expressing their feelings while staying in that accepting tone.)

You really wish you'd told me that you needed your jeans for today and are frustrated with yourself that you forgot and now angry with me that I didn't just have them done for you. (Help them to take responsibility for their part in this situation and gently, non-judgementally reflect how they are projecting their own feelings outwards on to you.)

I get it, I really do. (Repeat your acceptance of how they are feeling.)

I think we need to take some short time apart to cool down (take a step back from the heat of the situation to ensure that you stay in your own window of tolerance and can get them back into theirs by co-regulating them) *and then I'll help you find something else you feel comfortable in or you can call your friend and let her know that you can't come over anymore. I'll support you in either choice you make.* (Move into a solution-focused thought process while reinforcing that they can make a choice and the outcome is their responsibility – you won't be fixing this for them.)

Often these situations escalate because parents get pulled into the emotional demand of the child who is now setting the temperature of the interaction. *You* set the temperature gauge, *you* control the heat of the situation and that is how you stay effective and in control of these situations while attuning to and respecting your child's emotional experience in a validating, accepting and empathic way. This allows them to *get got* and *feel felt* by you.

HEIGHTENED SELF-AWARENESS

Middle childhood is a stage of development when children become more and more aware of themselves as individuals. That can be an intensely uncomfortable, overwhelming experience. Part of this increasing awareness is a desire to become more responsible and to take on and master more tasks for themselves. At the same time, they're hyper-critical of their own performance and fearful of failure, which can inhibit action and drive frustration with themselves. This is difficult to contain so spills over and out. One of the most effective ways to manage difficult, uncontainable emotions is to subject someone else to them, to project them onto someone else who can be a container for those icky and uncomfortable feelings they cannot hold in. Ideally, the *container* they choose is a solid, grounded, available attachment figure who can see what they are doing and how they are doing it and help them make sense of those feelings, breaking these down and slowly giving them back to them in more manageable bite-sized pieces (as detailed above).

Speaking of bite-sized pieces may bring back to mind how you parented your toddler. You will feel the echoes of early parenting responses in middle childhood, though that is not at all to say that you should treat your middle-childhood-stage child as though they were a toddler. Middle childhood is marked by significant personality and associated behavioural shifts. As mentioned above, the brain is in a phase of synaptic pruning, and running alongside this are erratic, unpredictable and inconsistent mood changes, when they swing wildly between showing you, their parents, affection and then disdain, and move sharply from feeling independent to feeling invisible. You will feel damned if you do and damned if you don't.

This stage of parenting can leave you languishing on the ropes but is really a call to action to invest in patience and empathy and remain open and available even, and perhaps especially, when your child is sending you a message that they do not want you around. (**Note:** Being available doesn't mean encroaching on their space and forcing yourself on them. Acknowledge you have heard them and state where you will be and that should they change their mind you would be happy to help them through this. Stay away but open and check back in after 15 minutes; if it's still no then walk away; 15 minutes later drop them a drink/small snack and smile and then walk away again without verbally engaging. Either this will be enough for your child to come down (emotionally speaking), as you are available and engaged without being insistent or intrusive, or they will now be able to accept your invitation to talk it through.

One of the hardest things about this phase of childhood is that your child must become more independent of you and shift their main focus from family to their peers *but* they cannot achieve this without your help and so it is vital that you know when to step in and take charge and when to step back and follow their lead and cues. This sounds easier than it is because thus far you and the family have been your child's greatest influence, but now they are moving out and into a much broader network of influence that you cannot fully control or manage for them, and they must do this for themselves.

To be successful here your child must draw on what they know in terms of being able to read and understand other people's points of view, thoughts, feelings, beliefs, desires and intentions. Social cognition is the term used to describe the ability to read social situations, and your child is developing a stronger sense of social cognition as they grapple with the communication skills to enable them to relate and function in the world around them with other people in everyday situations. To do this they need strong problem-solving, interpersonal, empathy and critical-thinking skills.

Remember that they start to develop these life skills and capacity for general civility during the three stages of developmental play, especially in stage two play when they are between three-and-a-half and five years old. It is not a case of them really nailing these complex social processes at four years old, *but* there is the opportunity for them to develop the capacity for these social skills to continue to grow and develop within them from that point forward. This is what is really increasing now, all of the opportunities they have had between three-and-a-half and five years old to develop their inner working model and sense of self (i.e. to understand themselves, the world and other people), provide the launch pad for them to jump off and out into the world on their own and manage social situations as individuals in their own right.

15-minute play that supports emotional resilience, critical thinking and empathy

Take a sheet of A4 or copybook paper. Start off by writing the first line of a story with *Once upon a time* (because once upon a time gives permission for anything to happen) and start the second line. Now fold down the first line and pass it over so that your child only gets to read the start of the second line. They must pick up from there and finish that line and start the next one. Then fold down the completed line and continue from the start of the next line. Continue this, passing the page over and back until you get to the end of the page. Whoever has the page at the bottom of it ends the story with the words *The End*. Now take the page back, unroll it and read it aloud while you both laugh and marvel at points of the story that are in or out of sync. Do not comment on handwriting or spelling or grammar or anything else like that – simply take it as fun story-building together.

Another activity is to write out themes and/or topics on scraps of paper that you mix in a bowl. Take turns picking one out and role-play being a newsreader reporting on that topic as a news story. Make it more challenging if they are at the older age and just put one word on the scrap of paper and tell them that they cannot use that word in their news report, but based on what they say the rest of you have to try to guess what word they are leaving out. They can give as much or as little detail as they choose. This will suit the children who tend to be more logical and grounded as much as those who have a flair for the dramatic, as they can report their news story in the style that best suits their temperament.

This type of narrative play is a great way to start practising tuning into the perspectives of others and reading their cues and prompts. It is fun and when something is fun we are more likely to stay engaged in it and to draw benefit from it. Just think about how you feel about the gym; if you enjoy it then I am betting it is something you make time to do, and if you do not you will find endless reasons to avoid it.

EMPATHY IS FEELING *WITH* PEOPLE

It is also at this stage of development that we want to find creative ways to reinforce empathy skills in our children. One of the best and most effective ways to help them build empathy is to show them empathy. Show them that you understand their feelings and even if you are not happy with the associated behaviour, you can understand with acceptance and empathy the feeling that lies beneath it and can reflect that understanding back to them in a way that helps them to make sense of their own feelings and understand that overt behaviour is underpinned by a physical and emotional state.

15-minute exercise

Do the *In your shoes* activity. When your child is emotionally spilling about what they have done/said or how they have experienced something, use your active listening skills. Let them speak without interruption or judgement. Take a deep breath and *agree with them*… yes, AGREE. You can say, 'When I put myself in your shoes I can understand why you think/feel/did this. It makes sense because you believed XYZ.' Now ask them to do the same for you. Invite them to 'Put yourself in my shoes and tell me why you think I might feel differently about this.' This is empathy building by encouraging the perspective taking of others and accepting their perspective as their truth. It is also encouraging some reflective space to calmly question our own beliefs and thoughts about something. And it is a great way to stay connected when correcting behaviour.

I also call this *trying on the feelings of others* in my therapeutic work with children of this age. I tell them a short scenario and ask them to try on the feelings of the person in my scenario and tell me how it feels from their point of view. Here is an example.

I'm going to tell you a story and as you listen I want you to picture the person I'm talking about in your mind. 'Once upon a time there lived a boy who had lots of brothers and sisters. His house was busy, loud and active. Sometimes his younger brothers and sisters would come into his bedroom to look at his stuff. One day he walked out of his house and just kept walking and walking. Suddenly he realised that he was quite far from home and didn't fully recognise where he was. It was quiet around him and there was lots of open space.' Now I want you to try on the boy's feelings and tell me what's happening in this story from his point of view.

You can make up any social scenario you want. It should be something relatable for your child but not so obvious that you are talking about something in their lives. Keep it short and avoid any judgements or feeling statements because you want them to project the feelings onto the story as they see/feel it. Another way to apply this type of activity is to go to the cinema together to watch a movie and afterwards take turns *trying on the feelings* of the various characters in the movie. You can do it with reference to a book your child is reading (I suggest that you read it too) or if you find that you spend a chunk of time each day in the car together, perhaps driving to and from school, suggest you listen to an audiobook together in the car each day and then at the end of each journey/day *try on the feelings* of a character. The key here is that you accept the perspective of your child as they try on the characters' feelings. It is not for you to say whether they are right or wrong to interpret it the way they do. *We must stay out of judgement if the goal is to teach empathy.*

Another great way to practise critical thinking is to bring up a (relatively) serious topic that is in the news/media and invite an open conversation and discussion about it. What do they understand about it, how do they think and feel, and then *wonder* if you were involved yourself, what actions you would do to change the situation. Accept their suggestion without judgement and further wonder how their suggestion would effect the desired change.

FINDING YOUR PARENTAL BOUNDARIES

In general, you will need to maintain limits and boundaries on what are acceptable ways to express their range of unpredictable and quite volatile emotions. Yes, you can feel this way but no, you cannot behave this way. Maintaining limits of the expression of emotions should not be confused or equated with punishment. You can maintain such limits in a gentle yet firm way by affording and at times directing time alone and away from the heat of the situation. Time alone can be in their room, with music, with a book, playing a sport, going for a walk, baking. This gives them the time and space to calm down and reflect on theirs and others' perspectives on a situation. It also gives you time, especially when you are feeling pushed close to or over your limits. Losing your temper and becoming overtly enraged with them is only adding fuel to the fire and will ensure that the heightened emotional state continues for a longer period of time.

Your ultimate parental power lies in staying calm, especially when staying calm is the hardest thing to do. Remember that one very effective way of dealing with our uncomfortable feelings is to project them outside ourselves and onto someone else who will serve as a container for what we cannot contain in ourselves. And so our children at this middle-childhood stage of development (and be warned as this will continue and indeed escalate beyond this stage into adolescence) will be compelled to project their uncomfortable feelings that they struggle to process and make sense of for themselves onto us. This is what is commonly referred to as *pushing our buttons*. Except, it isn't our buttons but theirs. How you stay in control of this is to try to stay calm, see what is happening and gently break down their feelings into more manageable bite-sized pieces and reflect those back to them: 'You are really angry because... You are yelling at me because you feel frustrated with yourself and want me to understand what that feels like for you.' Or, as I said, see it, feel it and buy yourself time to make sense of it yourself before you explode and yell back by suggesting some time alone (for both of you).

Now, I am not a fantasist when it comes to parenting, far from it, and this will certainly be a situation of *win some and lose some,* so be kind and forgiving to yourself and to your child. When it's not possible to stay calm and it does end in a screaming row upsetting everyone involved (note that I say when and not if, because this WILL happen), take the time and space needed afterwards to let the heat leave the situation (and people involved) and attend to your own feelings before you do the same with and for your child.

15-minute exercise: Taking care of yourself so that you can take care of them

Take a walk, stand out in the garden and just breathe or do a grounding exercise such as seeking and naming five things you can see around you, four things you can hear, three things you can touch, two things you can smell and one thing you can taste. You are connecting with the environment around but outside you and how it resonates within you. You are counting down 5, 4, 3, 2, 1 and focusing on your senses. This will help reset the brain (by changing your field of vision) and mindfully calm and ground you (the breathing and counting).

These things don't just work with children but with adults too. Once you feel grounded and calm, ensure that you have afforded your child some space to feel calm. Bear in mind that they are unlikely to have calmed down as much as you in this time because they are not an adult and don't have as broad a window of tolerance as we do. So once they have become calm, go back and engage in active repair. Reflect that things got out of control and be clear about how you felt in the moment, how you felt immediately afterwards, what you did to calm yourself down and how you feel now. Say, using short and succinct sentences, that you are sorry the discussion got out of control and ended up with so much yelling and that when your child feels ready you would like to try again in a calmer way.

Rupture is a part of every relationship, even the healthiest relationships, and so long as it is followed by experiential repair it will do no harm in your relationship, but in fact might enable an additional opportunity for growth and development of resilience.

Our pre-teen children tend to rely on their amygdala (the part of the brain where fight/flight/freeze emotional responses are processed) to process their emotions. Again, this will continue to be the case into adolescence. An adult brain will use the pre-frontal cortex to process most emotional experiences because by then we can (mostly and most of the time) *think our feelings and feel our thoughts*. This is not the case for middle childhood. Because they over-rely on the amygdala, their responses to emotional stimulus can be over the top, dramatic and largely dysregulated. I don't tell you this to make you feel better about them yelling or wailing at you, but more to help you understand it because knowledge is power. Your mature emotional right brain can reach out and seek to connect, co-regulate, accept and empathise with the immature emotional right brain of your child. It's a bit like throwing them an emotional rubber ring when they are drifting out to choppy seas, keeping them anchored to you until they can swim to shore for themselves.

CREATING YOUR PARENTAL SPACE

A sacrosanct part of parenting is protecting the parental space as much as you can. This is that space or time that is childfree and about the adults. This may well be a cup of tea and a chat with your partner once children are in bed or that essential cup of coffee and chat when a friend calls round and you dispatch your children to their own spaces so that you can enjoy yours. It can be hard enough to hold on to this space when children are really young because they seek to come to you every few minutes to show you what they did, to get help for something they want and to try to distract you from what you are doing to bring your focus back to them. This is often what I refer to as *a parental want clashing* with a child's need. You want your space and time and they need to keep you in their eyeline at all times and ensure that you are still there by constantly checking in with you. This isn't easy in early childhood parenting but you can understand it and even accept it. However, once they reach this age of 8–12 years we tend to expect that they can function for an hour without our constant attention and focus and can self-entertain while we take some time for ourselves with our own friends and conversations. When this isn't the case, it can be really frustrating and lead to tensions in the parent–child relationship.

Michelle booked in with me for some parental psycho-education work as she was struggling in her relationship with 10-year-old Meghan. She described a precocious and pseudo-mature girl. She felt that in the last 6–12 months Meghan had become 'too grown up' and yet still very immature. I asked her to give me an example of when this had happened. She spoke about a friend of hers calling round with her own child, who was two years younger than Meghan but with whom Meghan had previously played well.

On this occasion, she observed that Meghan refused to leave the kitchen where the adults were. She repeatedly found cause to come in to check with Mum about things that really didn't need checking. She was seeking snacks and drinks that Mum interpreted were simply 'faked to justify being in my space rather than in her own'. Mum had repeatedly redirected Meghan to the sitting room where the other child was playing, but Meghan had whined and said she didn't want to play with the other child, adding, 'I have nothing in common with her; I don't want to play what she does.' Mum was embarrassed and took Meghan aside and scolded her, insisting she play with the other child. Meghan then stormed into the sitting room and sat sulking on the floor. When they had gone home, Mum had gone in and told Meghan she was cross with how she had behaved. Meghan said, 'But I wanted to hang out with you guys and chat with you.' Mum felt very intruded upon and as if she couldn't have time with her adult company, as this was becoming a pattern. Even when she tried to have time with Dad or a conversation with Dad, Meghan was constantly 'lurking and eavesdropping'.

Meghan was what we call a pseudo-mature child. Actual maturity develops gradually over time and is about knowing yourself and what you stand for as a person and operating in accordance with your own beliefs. Pseudo-maturity is about trying to act and be like people who are older than you. Because it is not authentic and is moreover a form of play-acting whereby the overt behaviours are acquired from others rather than developed within the self, this pseudo-maturity can actually serve to block the emergence of authentic maturity. That being said, in this context it is not a clinical issue nor is it anything to really worry about. With appropriate boundaries and redirection it can be worked through.

Remember that this stage of development is marked by ego-centrism in the child too. As such, Meghan believed that the adults around her should be delighted she wanted to be part of their group and experienced their redirection as a rejection of her, resulting in overt sulking and pouting as she let her disappoint-ment be known. In this instance, I suggested that Mum and Dad ensure that they were checking in with Meghan over dinner as to what the best bit of her day was and what bit she wished she could change. I directed that the adults should also share their own best bit and what they would like to change. In this way, Meghan was an active part of the adult conversation but in a boundaried way.

Previously, Mum and Dad discussed their days together after Meghan had gone to bed. I also suggested that when Mum was having company she would direct Meghan *before* her friend arrived that she would be spending time with her friend in the kitchen and remind her that when Meghan has a friend over Mum does not hang around them all the time but gives them space to have their own conversations and fun. She would then assign a task to occupy Meghan (sometimes it would be to read a book, or make jewellery or to do some other arts/crafts activity). If the friend would be bringing a child with them, Mum should explain to Meghan that she would really appreciate it if Meghan would play with the child and show her how to do something that only someone Meghan's age would know (fancy hair braiding appealed a lot). And finally, I suggested that Mum assured Meghan that she would go for a walk, just the two of them, that evening (this was possible in their family but if it is not, pick a time when it will be and do it then). Equally, you could suggest going for a hot chocolate together at the weekend. This is something that appeals to the pseudo-mature child, as it feels quite adult to go to a café for a hot drink and piece of cake.

Beyond managing the overt behaviour of pseudo-maturity, I often think about what else it might be communicating to us. If a child is craving to be like the adults in their lives, what is something exclusive to adulthood that is not always a part of childhood? Independence! I suggest that when you see this pseudo-maturity start to emerge, take it as a sign that your child is ready for increased independence.

PLAY TIP: PRACTISE PARALLEL PLAY

Sometimes a child will seemingly struggle to know what they should do and will declare that they cannot play alone or just don't know what to do. This means they will keep coming to you to seek to stay with you or to demand that you sit with them and play with them. While this might be a lovely invite, it is not something you can do all day and also we do want to see more independence skills at this stage, including being able to play independently of you for periods of time. Parallel play can be a good way to achieve this.

- Start them off playing – sit with them for a few minutes and get the play going, then excuse yourself in the hope that they can continue the play.
- Set a task – 'I want you to do this jigsaw and then I'll come back' or 'Why don't you see if you can re-set up the dolls' house furniture and then I'll come in to see how it's going.'
- Build up their capacity slowly by sitting in the room with them but not actually joining in their play with them – you might sit and read a book on an armchair in the room they are playing in or have them sit alongside you while you both read your books. Find reasons to put your book down to leave the room and return, starting with small separations and building up.
- Praise their creativity and efforts but do not intrude on their play.
- Do not jump every time you are called by them – once you know they are safe, you know the demand for your presence isn't really needed, so you can say, 'I hear you. I'm doing something and will come to you when I'm done.'

You are gradually building up their capacity to self-motivate and self-entertain without them feeling abandoned or punished by your redirecting them away from you. Always be mindful of your tone of voice with this messaging. Keep your tone kind and encouraging and supportive of their endeavours. This redirection should never feel punitive. This will work best when you are still doing your parent–child 15 minutes of play each day as they will find the knowledge that you will be playing with them in a predictable and consistent way reassuring and it means they can trust your presence and not need to pull and demand and seek it of you as much.

THE BATTLE FOR INDEPENDENCE

This period in a child's life is a time of a parental want clashing with the child's need in that we want them to do as they are told and they need to push us out of their way to assert how they can do it themselves. This is when they will be embarrassed at you attempting to walk them to school and will insist they can do it themselves – when you reflect that you are not on board with this and will be walking them to school, they will walk 10 steps behind you or storm ahead acting as though they don't know you. Let them. So long as you can see them and reach them quickly, they are safe.

This is also when they start lecturing you on how your boundaries are misguided because *all of their friends are allowed* to do whatever it is they are seeking to negotiate. And this overt manipulation doesn't end here because they will conspire with their friends to have the friend ask you to let them do something, believing you will find it harder to say no to their friend. They will dispatch their friend to ask about sleepovers and other activities and will try asking you for something in front of their friends and yours, assuming that the presence of others will mediate the type of response you are likely to give. Just as when they were two years old, the task here is to hold the boundaries gently yet firmly in place while they push and rail against them.

A quick note on the subject of **sleepovers** because this is a topic that comes up a huge amount for me in my work with parents of children this age. This is really something you need to have a family policy on. You either do or do not do sleepovers. And either choice is okay. For some people, it does not feel comfortable to have other children (other than family members) sleep overnight, or to have their children sleep away from home in others' homes. It may be that the family routine is disrupted by them or that having younger children means this disruption is not possible to manage in your family. If this is you, then you say early and often, we do not do sleepovers in this family. This is your mantra and you will return to it often. If you are happy to facilitate sleepovers with friends, decide between you what age these should start at, whether they are limited to special occasions like birthdays or mid-term breaks and how they should be structured; for example, can they sleep out in a tent in the garden, must they be in the bedroom or can they sleep in sleeping bags on your sitting-room floor while watching movies late into the night? At what point do you say, lights out and go to sleep, or do you turn a blind eye as they talk into the night and are sleepy zombies the next day? Think it through so that you, the parent-in-charge, are setting the tone and holding the boundary on them rather than your child, who will happily take the lead and direct you as to how such things are practised.

It can be useful to have an open communication with the parents of your child's friends to ensure you are on the same page or at least clear about the lines on your page, but this doesn't mean you have to move on your own beliefs and parenting practices in this or any other regard. As you will often tell your child, *just because everyone else is doing it doesn't mean you have to* or, my own mother's preferred line, *if everyone else was jumping off a cliff, would you jump too?*

Your child seeking independence is not a negative thing – far from it – but managing it is key. You do this by affording them opportunity for independence from a young age and growing it up with them within the safety and security of your parental boundaries. It is really important that in becoming more independent your child does not assume a position of power within your family or even within your own parent–child relationship with them.

When the controlling child is internally out of control

Maura came to see me to discuss how she was feeling about her nine-year-old daughter Phoebe. She was emotional and very stressed out as she described how she was feeling 'bullied and manipulated' by her own daughter at home. She said that she had 'a street angel and house devil' because no one in her own family could believe what she was saying about Phoebe's behaviour towards her and that was also stressing her out as she felt as if they didn't believe her and that **she** was the issue, not Phoebe.

I asked her to give me examples of what she was describing. In doing so I was seeking to elicit what are called **relational episodes**, which are specific times that the described behaviour occurred. This allows me to get a sense of what is going on from the perspectives of all involved. It allows me to try on the feelings of all parties involved and also to observe how someone is feeling in the recalling of the memory. Is it something that they can recall from a position of fresh thinking and new perspective or in the retelling are they experiencing it as though it just happened?

Maura gave me an example of how Phoebe would come into the kitchen after school and ask what they would be having for dinner. Whatever Mum said was for dinner would be met with derision and disgust: 'I am NOT eating that – it's disgusting.' I wondered what would happen next. In the relational episode she shared she described how she would plate up dinner and then start to make something else for Phoebe. This meant that Maura rarely got to sit and eat with the rest of the family and would be making something from Phoebe's favourite menu each day.

I wondered where the resentment in Maura really lay – in Phoebe refusing her food (nurturing) or in Phoebe controlling when Maura got to eat her own dinner. I suggested that she remove the emotional charge around food by meal planning ahead of time and using a blackboard in the kitchen to write up what dinner would be for the week. If there were any objections to that dinner, there would be no other options because nobody gets to eat their favourite food every day of the week,

BUT Mum would ensure that every member of the family's favourite dinner was there once a week. I further suggested she gave some creative control to Phoebe rather than getting locked into a battle, so on a Friday she initiated the 'make your own dessert' routine. Maura would put out a couple of choices of ice cream and a variety of toppings for Phoebe and her siblings, who got to make up their own desert bowl as they wanted it for themselves.

On weekend mornings, she invited Phoebe to make her own smoothies whereby she could choose what she wanted to go into the blender and have it on her terms. Apart from this, dinner would be served and the family would sit and eat together. If Phoebe refused to eat she would still be expected to sit at the table while everyone else ate and talked together.

I suggested Maura plate up a small portion of dinner for Phoebe anyway and simply sit it on the table without any expectation that she had to eat it. By removing the emotional charge and having Phoebe sit, there was a chance she would eat some of it, but equally she couldn't assert that she wasn't given any dinner. It was important that Maura did not cook anything else for Phoebe but gently and firmly held the boundary. Phoebe was free to eat fruit from the fruit bowl if she was hungry.

Maura reported Phoebe persisting with not eating her dinners most evenings for the first two weeks of the new protocol. However, as she got used to having control over 'make your own dessert night' and 'weekend smoothie making' and Maura introduced 'make your snack for family movie night', Maura began to see small but growing changes in Phoebe around the dinners. She stopped rowing about it but sat pouting. Then she started picking at it, building up to eating it. It took four weeks for Phoebe to sit and eat her dinner properly with everyone, but along the way Maura just held the boundary and didn't comment either way on what she was doing – no criticism or *beseeching to eat and no praise when she did. This was vital to success in this instance.*

The key in managing independence lies in maintaining parental boundaries. You can invite independence into your child's life (and you should do so) without losing parental control – and remember that when I say parental control, you should never have to say the words 'I'm in charge' because as soon as you do, you are not in control. Being in charge/in control is about doing not saying, and if you are doing it, then you have no need to say it. Just as a two-year-old's job is to push and challenge the boundaries you lay down and it is your job to hold them gently yet firmly in place, this is also the case now. While a child may well seek to take control, if you give them too much control or too much power in the relationship, it will overwhelm and actually stress them out. Food and eating is an area where we tend to see such dynamics played out because in a world where 8–12-year-olds crave independence, they remain mostly dependent on their parents-in-charge for most things in their life. However, with food, what goes in/out of the body is (with rare exception) fully in their control. This was the case with Maura and Phoebe. We had to remove the high emotional charge around food and eating in their relationship and create more appropriate opportunities for Phoebe to have control in her life and practise independence.

Retreating from the world – hiding behind parental dependence

Paul came to see me with his parents, who believed that he was lacking confidence and was very shy and withdrawn. Shyness is not a cause for clinical concern unless it is having a pervasive impact on the quality of someone's life. Paul had begun to drop his extracurricular activities, hadn't invited friends over for a long time and his parents feared he was regressing in terms of things he used to be able to do for himself but now couldn't or wouldn't. He seemed to need their help and assistance with everything.

The first time they arrived in my clinic rooms I observed with interest how Paul's parents helped him to take off his coat and placed it on the coat hook for him. They directed him where to sit and even made suggestions as to what he would like to play with. They were kind in their tone and very caring towards him in doing so. However, this was a nine-year-old boy who appeared and was reported to be physically strong and capable, and I wondered why he wasn't doing these things for himself. I suggested that his parents sit outside and that Paul and I had some time to ourselves.

I showed him around the room and what was there and invited him to choose something he would like to play. I could see that he was looking at something on a shelf and I said, 'You can take that down if you'd like.'

He hesitated and said he didn't think he could reach it and asked that I do it. I agreed that the shelf may be a little out of his reach but wondered what he could do to get it for himself anyway. He looked at me as if he was surprised and didn't know what to do. And so we sat. Thinking. Looking at the item on the shelf. After about 10 minutes (trust me it felt longer) he got up, walked over, stretched up on his tippy toes and raised his arms high up and, sure enough, he could then quite comfortably reach the item he wanted for himself.

I praised his efforts: 'Paul, you really wanted that item and I could see that you took time to work out how you would reach it for yourself and you came up with stretching. I like that you tried that for yourself.'

I met with his parents after a few sessions that all went quite like this and I learned more about Paul at home. His parents still viewed him as a very young child and conceded that they were still doing a lot of things for him that he could do for himself. We started making changes here, small changes that really did have a big impact. We then said that Paul would do one after-school activity per week that would be non-negotiable, but he would get to choose the activity himself from a list of three that his parents were happy were suitable, affordable and manageable for them. I asked that they give Paul chores and an agreed small amount of pocket money each week which he would be entirely responsible for and they would not seek to tell him how he should or should not spend it. Paul's confidence grew and quite quickly he re-engaged with his peer group and, as his parents put it, he found his happy part again.

Having plenty of developmentally appropriate opportunities to practise independence helps to boost positive life skills and is also an essential part of building self-esteem in your children. This is a difficult age where self-esteem and confidence are under attack, where fitting in with peers is of the utmost importance to your child. It is also a time of intense change when they have to relearn who they are and what they are about. Your previously bubbly and overtly happy young child can suddenly lose some of that outward shine as their self-esteem takes a dip. Getting to walk to the local shop, or being in charge of their own pocket money, being able to make and take appropriate choices and decisions for themselves are all really good ways to grow independence and self-esteem in your child. You are communicating that you trust the child, that you believe they are capable of doing something for themselves, and it gives you the opportunity to offer them positive feedback and praise their efforts over any outcomes.

OTHER WAYS TO SUPPORT YOUR CHILD'S SELF-ESTEEM – A TIP LIST FOR PARENTS

- **Ask questions** such as: 'I wonder how that would feel if someone said that about you' or 'I wonder what you would do if you knew someone was being bullied or you were being bullied yourself.' This encourages your child to consider the perspectives of others and to engage with their internal feeling states in experiences.

- Shine a light on the **good behaviours**: Ask yourself how you celebrate achievement in your family. You want your child to know when they have done well and to know how proud you are of everything they achieve and try to achieve, regardless of outcome.

- **Good enough is good enough**: Set realistic and achievable expectations of your child and let them know how much you believe in their ability to do well and to ultimately do their very best, which will be different for each child. Ask yourself if you want your child to do *their* best or *your* best.

- **Be interested in them and their lives**: Stay engaged in what is going on and whom they are friends with. Start young with asking what the best bit of their day was and which bit they wish had gone differently. A few days later, refer back to this and ask them how that thing they were dealing with worked out; this shows that you are holding them and their lives in mind. Get your child to play their favourite music for you or teach you the games they like to play, meet their friends and have them over to your house. Try to find something fun that you and your child can enjoy doing *together*.

- **Focus on behaviour not the person**: Be clear about what you are saying, for example '*Don't* do… *because* of… try doing... *instead*. It makes me so happy when I see you're listening to me and doing your best, so thank you!'

- **Be liberal with your compliments and praise** and do so **without conditions**: Instead of 'That was a good effort for your first time', simply say, 'You were great. I could see how hard you were trying and it made me feel so proud of you.' Teach your child to accept and give compliments freely; this means doing the same yourself as they take their lead from you. Don't dismiss a compliment such as, 'You look really good,' with, 'Oh this old thing, I've had it ages.' Simply say, 'Thank you.' With children, try not to compliment only looks or appearance, so instead of, 'You look pretty, that's a nice dress,' say, 'You look like a very clever girl. I wonder what book you're reading right now.'

- Gradually **give your child (age-appropriate) responsibility**: This encourages trust and independence, which in turn build self-esteem and confidence. It is important that we allow children to make mistakes – it is how they learn and it shows them that we believe in them. Again, this is a gradual and age-appropriate process.

- **Give your child (age-appropriate) responsibility at home**: Try giving them a chore or something they are responsible for doing that benefits the whole house/family. This teaches them that they are capable, valuable and a contributing member of the family. Feeling useful and needed is a very powerful way to feel good about yourself.

A big job of this stage of development is, as I've now mentioned a few times, to develop and deepen an emotional vocabulary, to expand on the ways your child can express how they are feeling so that they don't withhold heightened emotion that will become trapped without a means of release. Trapped emotion can cause a range of physical and psychological issues.

Have you ever heard yourself ask your child 'How are you feeling?' I am quite sure you have. What kind of responses does this elicit? Well, likely it will range from a dismissive or closed off sounding statement such as, *'Fine, I dunno, why are you asking me that?'* to a more angry tone of reply such as, *'I feel ANGRY and here's why I feel that way… [leading to the child going on the attack]'* and many more responses in between. The healthiest way to develop an inner-emotional world that leads to a sense of felt safety and an ability to link overt behaviour to underlying emotional states is to invest in developing a rich emotional language and creative, positive ways of expressing those emotions so that the child can grow to understand themselves from the inside and outside (how they experience themselves and how others experience them). This technique works really well when your child (note that I said *when* and not *if* because this will definitely happen, time and again!) is specifically angry or upset over something that has happened (not a generalised feeling but in response to one specific thing). I find it to be a really nice and effective technique for expressing how you are feeling in a creative and playful way.

Twelve-year-old Shane's parents were frustrated that he wouldn't open up to them; they felt that they had no insight into how he was feeling about anything. They described him as moody and angry and they felt powerless to help him because he wouldn't express any feelings to them, but his overt behaviours were having a really negative effect on the family. As a part of his treatment we did this exercise.

Shane was angry that his parents had said he couldn't have a mobile phone until he was in secondary school (one year away).

Me: When your parents refused to give you the phone you felt… (I invite just one word).

Shane: *Angry.*

Me: What colour is that feeling?

Shane: *Red.*

Me: *What is the physical sensation of this feeling?*

Shane: *(paused to think – this was good, as it meant he was reflecting inwards to wonder about how it felt) It's pins and needles.*

Me: *If that feeling were an animal, what animal would it be?*

Shane: *A lion.*

Me: *When you see that lion, what's the scene around it?*

Shane: *(paused to think about this one. This also showed he was starting to become more reflective) It's a very large field, nothing but land all around. There are no trees and no one else around.*

Me: *How does the lion move through the field you're describing?*

Shane: *He runs very, very fast in all directions but it all looks the same so it's a bit like he's running around in circles instead of a big open field.*

We paused and I wondered what that was like for Shane to picture his feelings about something. He said he had thought it was stupid at first but when he tried to picture the scene, the animal that was in it made him feel sad instead of angry and he had thought he might cry and didn't know why. We sat with that and thought about how sometimes we think we have one feeling but that feeling might be hiding another feeling. We reflected on how that lion must have felt alone in that big field, running so fast but not getting anywhere.

Shane suddenly started to talk to me about how he felt like that with his parents and that talking with them made him feel as if he was banging his head on a wall (he sometimes actually did bang his head on a wall in anger). I empathised how frustrating that must feel and wondered if he thought his parents understood that. He was certain they didn't, so I said, 'Well, that way really isn't working for you. I wonder if we can *try a different way for you to express how you're feeling in a way that gets heard and keeps you out of trouble.'*

*Getting Shane to visualise his feelings in a removed but relatable way gave him the required distance to be able to make better sense of what was happening inside him and how he could find more effective ways of explaining it. I met with his parents and shared this technique with them so that they could use it at home with him. In doing so, they were meeting him at the level of how his feelings **felt** for him and helping him to link his feelings to how he was behaving and to gradually begin to use words rather than actions to express his emotional states. The added value here was in how his parents learned to respond to his feelings within this exercise, such as wondering about what would help the lion to find his way out of the feeling when in that big field or wondering what shade of red the colour is or what might slow the lion down or change the vibrancy or intensity of the colour or feeling in the moment.*

HOW TO BE AN INFLUENCER – YOUR CHILD'S INFLUENCER, THAT IS

In an ever-increasing digital age where YouTubing is a career and social influencer is a lucrative occupation, how do we ensure that we are the main influencers in our children's lives? We will not be the only influence, that is for certain, but in a world where children are the target demographic of marketing companies from infancy upwards, what do we need to do to make sure that ours is the message they default to in times of choice and questioning? It is hard to be a lone parental voice amidst the roar of mass media. So how do we manage the influence of the influencer?

A study in *Adweek* magazine[4] stated that by the age of three years old, children in the USA could recognise 100 different brands. This is not a phenomenon exclusive to the USA by any means. The article to which I refer goes on to quote a former marketing consultant to Hasbro, Mattel and Nestle who said: 'Babies don't distinguish between reality and fantasy, so they [companies] think, "Let's get them while they're susceptible".'

You are not just buying a book for your child because that branded book is automatically nudging and directing your child towards the TV show, computer game, pencil case, playing cards, lunch box and so on that go with it. The commercialisation of childhood and play is big business and we, as parents, have to find a way to get our voices heard as we try to wade through all of that influence.

Just to state from the outset, I do see and believe that social-media influencers can have pro-social benefits for young people in terms of inspiring them to behave in more positive ways (I'm thinking of JoJo Siwa and her anti-bullying messages). However, in order to earn a living from what they do they are also marketing to our children… and via our children to us (I'm still thinking of JoJo Siwa and her range of hair bows).

It used to be our teenagers but increasingly it is our pre-teens who are spending large amounts of time online and on social-media platforms especially. Marketing companies are wise to this phenomenon and are quick to take advantage of this sitting audience, bombarding them with ads and sponsored content #ad #sponcon and because of the trust-based relationship, children form bonds with the influencers they follow. They (mostly) do not critically evaluate the ads or products those influencers are selling to them.

So how do we ensure it is our voice, our message and our moral compass/guidance that they default to rather than these other external influences? We have to start conversations early and keep having them. We cannot afford to talk about the difficult topics once and then exhale, thinking, *phew, that's that topic boxed off.* We need to revisit the topics and grow the content of those conversations up in line with our children growing up. We need to keep the door of communication always open and work to convey the message that nothing is off limits with us – they can come to us to talk about anything and we are open to going there (wherever that might be) with them.

Pester Power – don't let it wear you down!

We can start by delaying the point of access to social media for our children in middle childhood until they are in their adolescence (or for as long as possible). The middle-childhood brain is still too immature to manage social media in a healthy way with sensible boundaries. There are plenty of examples of adults who struggle to use social media in a healthy way, so of course our young and neurologically developing children struggle to regulate themselves online or to modulate the impact social media has on their everyday real lives.

Middle childhood is a time when, developmentally, our children have key, egocentric motivations. They want to be **popular** and to be liked by their peers. This can correlate to a need to gather huge numbers of followers/likes/endorsements online, leading them to say yes to anyone who wants to follow them just to build up numbers.

They are susceptible to the intense attention a stranger may afford them online and vulnerable to compromising their own boundaries in order to not offend that person whom they now believe to be their friend, and this can lead to all kinds of reckless online sharing and behaviours. Their focus is **on the self**, their clothes, style and interests, with a high emotional charge on the physical body. This leaves them vulnerable to feelings of not quite measuring up to the ideals perpetuated by the people (especially celebrities and influencers) online.

Social media makes celebrities suddenly very accessible; we can see their intimate family and personal life photos and can even directly communicate with them (the excitement if they happen to message us back!). Being so directly accessible makes them very real and relatable. Except, of course, they are not and it is very difficult for the middle-childhood brain to understand all of the filters, how many photos were taken before this one was selected and how contrived *all* content actually is, and see it for what it is. Further, because this phase of development is so subsumed with **developing a sense of self** and establishing the child as different from you, their parents, they are experimenting with identity, they are unsure and uncertain and oscillating wildly between one emotional state and another while they seek to work out what fits them. This quest for independence is complicated by this changeable behaviour whereby it seems they are actually regressing rather than surging forward.

Parentally we are also moving out of that secure stage of knowing *my child would never do that* to suddenly cringing with the realisation that *I can't believe my child did that*. They are impulsive and unpredictable yet we must strive to be calm and consistent.

Their brain is in that phase of reorganisation, synaptic pruning and starting to rewire itself for high impulsivity, risk-taking and poor judgement, so this is a time when opening up a world of social media and all that it brings in its wake can be dangerous. It is also a time when they will endlessly nag and seek to wear down our resolve to give them access to that world. And you know what? **Pester power** works! It's effective because we will slowly begin to question our stance on this topic the more they assert *everyone else can access it*. We will think that we can give them access via our old handsets without a sim card and it only works with Wi-Fi and we are supervising them. All true, all valid but regardless of the validity, that social-media world is opening up to our children, and we just hope that we have read it right and they are ready for it.

Although I sound foreboding, there are reasons for my caution here. One is the facts about brain development and high impulsivity and that social media simply wasn't developed with children of this age and stage of development in mind. It is designed for entertainment; there is no 'learning' value to it that cannot be better achieved offline via reading or in relation to you. Add this to what we know about the algorithms social-media platforms use and exchange with others, and how the younger they get access to your child, the more detailed the digital profile they build and the more specific the content driven at your child becomes. Your child's impulsive nature, combined with the compulsivity that social media elicits from so many of us (you think not? Start checking your social-media platform usage on your phone wellness app and it is quite a humbling experience), means they will struggle to regulate the time they spend online. With extensive and prolonged online time comes an impact on the all-important peer relationships that develop at this age. They really need to learn those important social skills that can only be learned intersubjectively, i.e. in real life with another person/people.

MY FIVE TOP TIPS FOR MANAGING SOCIAL-MEDIA ACCESS

What can you do to manage this phase as best you can, even when you do manage to delay the point of access until the end of middle childhood? I suggest a gradual introduction to these types of platforms regardless of the age you grant access.

- Grant access via your handset in your presence for a limited period of time and observe the impact this has on your child's behaviour and emotional state.
- Open a family account that you can all share access to and you can see how and what they post and respond to others.

- Follow their accounts – when you do grant access, ensure that it is on the basis that you are one of their friends/followers.
- Only allow access on a large screen such as a desktop or laptop in a family room rather than on small hand-held personal devices. This ensures openness, in that you can float around the space without hovering, and keeps your child more connected with you while online.
- Make digital access contingent on two real-life factors – they must spend 15 minutes a day with you and they must be spending time with their friends in real life once or twice a week (outside school). This can be at a shared activity or time spent in one another's homes or simply heading off for a walk together or meeting in a public park. We know that teenagers who have strong, healthy relationships with their family members and friends do best in adolescence so this is a very important factor in embarking on the social-media journey.

This is about you controlling social media rather than social media controlling your relationship with your child. There are definitely pro-social benefits to online life and social media, but those benefits can only be realised within a boundaried access system that is mindful of your child's development and respectful of family relationships.

WHEN SOCIAL MEDIA BECOMES VERY UN-SOCIAL

Caroline (11 years old) was brought to see me because her parents had been called up to her school to discuss some concerns they had about her actions on social media. Another parent had reported Caroline for cyber-bullying her daughter online via a social-media platform her parents hadn't been aware she was on. They themselves hadn't even heard of it and spoke of having minimal knowledge about social media and smart technology.

When we reflected on how Caroline had started to engage with social media, her parents spoke about how Caroline had purchased her first smartphone (she was on her third handset at this time) at seven years old when she had been gifted a large sum of money around her First Holy Communion. Her parents felt that they couldn't stop her buying the phone as it was her own money, and as they had such limited awareness of social media and technology they looked on it as a positive that she would develop digital literacy at a young age. This meant that she had largely unsupervised access to social media (though they did limit the amount of time she spent on her phone, it wasn't on their radar to monitor what she looked at when online). They were shocked and deeply distressed by what they had discovered and didn't know how to deal with this.

Caroline was defensive and angry when I sat down with her. She had lost access to her phone on the day her parents had been called up (three weeks before I got to meet with her) and she hadn't had it back since. She felt punished unreasonably and that her parents didn't care about how she felt about all of this. I acknowledged how hard this must feel for her and wondered about what she was doing with her afternoons and evenings now she didn't have her phone. She pouted at me that she was doing nothing and was bored. Again, I simply accepted this as her truth and empathised that this must be difficult, to simply sit still and not move.

I let that hang between us and she ventured, 'Well, not NOTHING nothing. I read books and I like to draw so I do some art.'

This gave me an in to explore the types of actions that gave her pleasure and helped her feel calm.

I decided not to mention the phone or what happened for the first three weeks as I really needed to focus on building a relationship with her so that she would feel she could open up about what had happened without it feeling as if I was another person disappointed in her or her behaviour. After three weeks, I simply wondered if she had got access to her phone yet. She sighed and put her head in her hands and said, 'No, I don't think I'll be getting it back because of what I did.' From here she could talk about what had happened and I learned the story through her eyes and thinking. She really didn't think she had done anything wrong – she absolutely couldn't see it.

Caroline had written some nasty comments under a school friend's posts online. These comments were specific to how the other child looked, what she was wearing and the type of pose in the other child's selfie. She was defensive when she spoke of this to me and I reflected that she sounded angry, but I was also feeling that she might be confused because it didn't seem as if she knew why her actions were wrong or why she was being punished. She sighed and said, 'I mean, I was trying to HELP her. She looked ridiculous and I was giving her advice about what to wear and how to pose so she didn't.'

From this perspective, I could empathise with Caroline's confusion and anger. She really did not see her comments as hurtful. We spent some time putting ourselves in her friend's shoes and what logging back on might have been like for her. To really help her to get it, we role-played it. She was herself and I was her friend. I reflected excitement at posting and then logging back onto my account, and as I sat and silently stared at my phone I simply let my facial expression change to show disappointment, sadness and embarrassment and modelled deleting the photo and crying. Caroline sat and watched me and stayed silent afterwards. A good five minutes of this silence passed and she whispered, 'I never thought about it like that. She must have felt awful.'

We spent another six weeks doing some intense empathy work with Caroline and also topping up her stage two play. You might recall from book one that stage two play is story-based type of play, where the four-year-old child starts to use small-world play or take two toys and have them talk to each other. The reason I was revisiting this stage with Caroline is that this is the stage of play whereby young children begin to acquire a capacity for empathy, critical thinking, reciprocity and general civility. When I talked with Caroline's parents I learned she hadn't really done too much of this type of play and had preferred TV and screen-based devices and art and crafts at this age. I modified the stage of play to meet Caroline's developmental age now.

This intervention was very successful with Caroline but I also talked with her parents about a number of the feelings and empathy exercises detailed here to playfully keep this skill developing in her as she grew. We also spoke about boundaried screen access and how her parents needed to get more informed and engaged with her social-media use. Caroline was able to make repair with her friend and wrote her a lovely card and a gift that she dropped round to her to say she was sorry for making her feel badly. The girls got back on track almost immediately after this point.

Modifying stage two play for older children

The three stages of developmental play are not just nice or good for children to experience, they are vital for developing a sense of self, an awareness of others and the world outside and around them. These stages of play lay the groundwork for all later psychosocial development, and gaps in any of the stages will emerge in overt behaviours that are problematic for your child later on. It is important that we see where those gaps are and return to that place to close the gap. However, if your 10-year-old child is showing signs of needing access to more sensory play, finger-painting may not be appealing to them and moreover may make them feel babyish, which will cause them to resist the intervention and render it useless.

What follows now are some practical play tips for modifying the type of play at each stage so that you can top up this type of play even though your child is older. If you are concerned that your child shows significant gaps or you are uncertain as to where the gaps lie, I advise you to refer to a suitably trained and certified child psychotherapist/mental-health professional who can assess and support you and your child with this. It is also important to note that a gap in one of these stages of play might not (probably won't to be honest) derail your child's development *but* it may feel like trying to walk around with a pebble in your shoe. Sure you can walk, but it's a little uncomfortable and if you keep walking with the pebble in there it is likely to cause you a blister that will lead to more pain and problems and difficulties with walking. It is better to pause, take off the shoe and shake out that pebble so that you can get back and stay on track and that walking becomes comfortable and manageable for you.

15-minute play solutions for using narrative play with your pre-teen

Story cubes: I've mentioned using these in other ways for developing narrative and empathy skills. I used them with Caroline by stacking the dice in a tower as we told our story. By doing this we could continue the story up and down each side. This is more challenging and thereby engaging for an older child as it requires a capacity for prolonged engagement and focus, as we stay connected in the story for a longer period of time. Story cubes are also a great way to support an older child to start reading and responding to the cues in others so that they can adapt their thinking and feeling and use critical thinking and emotional awareness to stay connected for longer periods of time.

Story stemming: Typically I do this using small-world dolls (such as dolls' house dolls) to play out the beginning of a social story, asking the child to show me how the story ends. I adapted this with Caroline by reading out the beginning of a social story. I had written one for her to be relatable to her experiences and world views but not identical to her own – a degree of separation is helpful so that it's not so obvious it is about the child per se. I then offered her a choice of different endings that I had written out on cards and laid out for her to read and asked her to choose the one that she felt was most appropriate. We then paused and reflected on this ending and how the various characters felt and responded to the ending. Then I challenged her by removing her ending and imposing an alternative one that was quite different to how she chose to end the story. I asked her to tune into how my ending to the story made her feel, how it might make the characters in the story feel and how they would now have to adapt their behaviours and feelings around the new ending. This is a spin on the old *choose your own ending* mystery story books that were popular in the 1990s. However, it really calls on a child this age to dig deep into their resources to manage the arousal level while holding multiple perspectives in mind and then to do that in an uncomfortable ending that is not of their choosing, because in life we don't always get to control the outcomes of events and experiences.

The director game: Another useful activity to playfully engage a child on serious and uncomfortable events is to tell them that what has happened is a movie and they are the director of that movie. As director, they get to yell 'CUT' at any point they like and edit the scene to bring about a different ending or interaction between characters. With Caroline, I used this activity a number of times. She felt both challenged and empowered by it, and this was a very insightful provocation with her as it is helpful to see how a mild level of stress changes a child's behaviour and actions. Her initial director effort was to show dominance over the adults who sought to hold her accountable.

If I were president of the world the first three things I would do/ change are: This is an interesting projective activity to playfully explore dynamics of power and selfish versus selfless actions. It is important that you don't pass judgement on anything your child chooses as their three action points but reflect with curiosity on how that would affect *them, others and the world.* If helpful and to make this more interactive, you can also choose your three actions and use this as a way of doing rather than saying how a more empathic set of actions would have a potentially greater and more positive impact.

The benefits of imaginative and narrative-based play

The imaginative and narrative-based play our children typically start to develop around three-and-a-half to four years old and immerse themselves in up to five years old still has strong developmental benefits through middle childhood. (There will still be elements of this stage of play evident as they move into stage three – dramatic role play – beyond five years old but before it is observed to be the dominant way of playing.) This is especially true when our children in middle childhood are relearning themselves and evolving in their development to move away from parents and family as their greatest influence and look to peers and others instead. They are attracted to the influence of others but still developing the skill set that enables them to assess and filter through what is appropriate behaviour. It is not unusual for us therefore to experience our children suddenly act in ways that we previously would have asserted with confidence they would never do. They are no longer who they once were but are still learning how to be in the world and how to be with and around others. Keeping empathy, critical thinking and problem-solving skills an active part of how we parent them allows us to stay playfully engaged and connected while also having a road map to navigate them (and ourselves) out of the choppy waters they may (and indeed will) veer into.

Key learnings from Caroline's story

This stage of development is so important that as parents, we must show (with actions not just words) that *we are interested in what interests our children.*

Caroline's parents had little to no interest in smart technology or social media. Because of this they were not invested in it or even in learning about it and stayed on the outside of the world that held great intrigue and interest for her. This left her alone and isolated in an ever-evolving environment where she could be heavily influenced by others without her parents, her emotional safe haven, to support and co-regulate her through. This experience not only afforded Caroline an opportunity to learn about how her words and actions had consequences for both herself and others, but it also afforded her parents the opportunity to see and feel through the impact of their disconnect with her at a time when repair and recovery is a lot easier. Had this continued into her adolescent years when developmentally she would withhold more from her parents, they would have likely experienced bigger challenges and also greater difficulty reaching and reconnecting with her.

Creating a parent action plan for Caroline

1. I advised Caroline's parents to book a consultation with a staff member of a phone shop and get a tutorial talking them through the capacity of the handset they were giving their daughter and also sit with someone who was social-media savvy and become more informed about that too (both could easily name someone in their circle who was well placed to do this with and for them).

2. I suggested they open a family social-media account where they each get to pick five people/accounts that their shared account would follow (this allows each of them to learn more about what interests each other but also enables them to gain even deeper insight into who interests their daughter).

3. They could all sit together and spend time scrolling and discussing what they see, questioning photos that look really staged and considering intended and unintended messages behind the posts. This last point is an important one at this stage of development because it is very challenging for Caroline's age group to critically assess what they see, generally trusting all the influencers they follow and accepting the content as real and true. Her parents could wonder what she thought and felt about an image; they could actively listen and reflect what they heard her say, then offer how they thought and felt about the same image, perhaps bringing to Caroline's attention some aspect she hadn't previously considered.

4. I also suggested they create screen-free zones in their home (bedrooms, the dining room, the kitchen, the bathroom) and boundaries around when phones should be switched off (8 p.m. to 8 a.m. every day). Limit-setting was an important step towards helping Caroline to engage safely and in a healthier way with the phone and social-media platforms.

There was learning for all of them in these exercises but underpinning that learning was *connection*, thereby creating an opportunity for *shared learning* so Caroline wouldn't feel lectured and preached at and they wouldn't feel clueless about what they were talking about.

For your behavioural correction to be effective, it is always best to start by securing emotional connection.

CHAPTER 7

How Do I Get My Child to…
Answers to the Questions I'm Most Asked by Parents

THE MAKE IT FUN TO GET IT DONE APPROACH!

In my clinical experience, the questions I most commonly hear from parents all begin with *How do I get my child to do…* (fill in the dots yourself). Is there anything more frustrating than when you are trying to *get* your child to do something they simply don't want to do? My answer to these questions generally starts with some variation of 'You have to make it appealing, make it fun', which may well be frustrating too until you link it to some practical ideas.

One of the most common ones I hear is about **exercise**.

Question: How do you get your child to engage in physical activity when they hate exercise… or at least they currently think they hate it?

Answer: We know from all of the health research that if a parent is unhealthily overweight then their child is much more likely to be so themselves. That's not about blaming, but rather flip that thought on its head and consider the positive influence you can also have on your child's attitudes to health and well-being. If you can have this big an influence, use that influence to effect positive change by leading with positive example yourself. Pause right now and consider your own attitude to exercise and physical activity. How does your child see you approach, think and speak about exercise? Is it something you put off, complain about, speak about in a problem-focused way or see as something you *have* to do rather than *choose* to do? The first step to change how your child feels about it is to change how you feel about it, if this is the case.

Alternatively, if you adore exercise and see it as something to be militantly followed and adhered to in a regimented way, your attitude and approach may be experienced as something your child feels they must endure rather than embrace with enthusiasm. In acting out some resistance to you as they developmentally begin to explore their independence more and seek to differentiate themselves from you, they may well resist the thing that you feel so strongly about – exercise.

And if the activity was something they loved to do and you watched them engage in so willingly with enthusiasm as a younger child, show great skill at and progress at a competitive level within but now they have decided to suddenly drop it, it can be very frustrating and confusing for you. Sometimes when the fun is taken away and it becomes about training and achieving and competing, children lose interest because it has become more work than play. Might this be the aspect they are resisting? And just to really confuse you, some children, especially the older ones, are quite motivated by such goals and targets and achievements and thrive on competitive training.

You will know which approach or path of resistance best suits or describes your child.

Generally, younger children are motivated by fun and play-based physical activity rather than classic exercise. Consider outdoor play but add in activities like chasing, rounders and tip the can; design an outdoor challenge-based assault course that involves balancing, jumping, crawling, hopping, climbing, running, and time each other.

Children in middle childhood tend to enjoy physical activity more if their friends can participate as well. Consider activities such as having them and their friend take your dog for a walk, or plan a lengthy hike in some local hills/forest area and have them invite a friend or two along and let them walk a bit ahead of you so they can engage with their friends rather than you. As a family, plan an orienteering activity. I especially like this for this age group because orienteering is a great way to build cognitive skills with the decision-making aspect, engage problem-solving skills with map reading, and physical exercise with walking, climbing and jumping. You can increase the level of challenge (and thereby make it more engaging for older children in this stage of development) by adding a timing aspect, or make it a mini-competition to see who can work out clues fastest or get to checkpoints fastest. In orienteering, you must navigate a series of checkpoints that you locate by reading a map and making a series of decisions and choices as to what is the best and quickest/safest route. Start really simple and design your own map that would get you and your children navigating in your own familiar area. Reach out to your local orienteering club – you don't have to join if that is not an option (such as if it is too far away) – but ask them for tips and suggestions to get you going. Celebrate everyone working together to get round with home-made hot chocolate or some such treat afterwards.

Other things to try with children this age that use fun to get it done include the following:

Use spontaneity: Have a ball in your hands and call everyone into a shared space (telling them to hit pause on whatever they are doing for 15 minutes). Without too much fanfare or explanation, immediately begin a group game of donkey/horse. This is the game where you have to toss the ball to each other and if the person drops it they get a letter of the word DONKEY or

HORSE (whatever version you are playing) and the one who spells the word first is out, with last person standing the winner. Make this more interesting and have everyone stand on one leg hopping while you wait for the ball to be thrown around; then mix it up by changing to jumping or waving arms above heads while they wait – this also calls for quick reflexes to move to catch the ball as it comes to them. Keep it safe by saying you must ensure eye contact before throwing and emphasising you throw it *to* someone and not *at* them. This will give you all a 15-minute burst of activity without having had to apply too much planning. Alternatively, get a game of Twister and have it set up when they come in and say that the Wi-Fi will go back on after you've all played a game for 15 minutes together.

Set the timer: Say that you all have to take turns doing 15 minutes of squats, burpees, lunges, star jumps and crunches (in total, not 15 minutes per exercise) and cheer each other on. Being each other's cheerleaders can help them to do it because they will feel that they are helping you to do it. Sometimes I use activity dice – two dice in different colours; one dice has exercises written on each side and the other has reps from 5–30 (you can make your own and use minutes on this other cube from one to five minutes per exercise).

Take a jog or long walk together: Use this as your way of also spending some one-to-one time together and getting outside. Basically take a do-it-together approach.

Structure it: Sometimes a bit of structure helps get you all started and keeps you on track. Make a calendar of planned physical activities and write them up on your family activity chart. Focus on a small activity each day and one larger-scale (like a family hike or orienteering) activity once a week.

Chart the activity and when you did it and get everyone to give it a star rating so you can get some feedback as to what feels like fun and what doesn't. Equally, make an activity jar and fill it with lots of pieces of paper that all have a different activity written on them. It is like a lucky dip, and you take turns to pick one out, which is then the activity you do.

Work towards a goal: This could be that you all sign up for one of those outdoor mud-run events that you complete together or for a 5km or even a 10km run that you must get out and train for bit by bit each day. You can add an element to this by committing to raising money for charity in doing it, as this way you will be kept on track both by the goal and the cause.

Time it right: Make sure you schedule or suggest the activities for a key time of day. For some of us, that will be stopping by the park on the way home from school to get some busy and active play done together. This is a good way to shake off the day too, so that when you get home everybody is calmer as a result. For others of us, it will be after dinner when the whole family are together and you can do some active play or activities or a nice long walk before bedtime. Work out what suits the rhythm of your family and start with that.

Share the responsibility in a fun way: Take turns rotating who gets to pick the activity for the family. Your children might be signed up to individual activities or their own team activities during the week (great, keep those up) but build in a tradition of at least one fun family active activity each week, and that's the one to rotate.

Keep it local and keep it free (ish): Your kids may be tempted to pick something fun and exciting but perhaps costly (something like wall-climbing or the local gym or trampolining centre) so consider setting a boundary that there can only be one costly activity per month (or every six weeks, depending on what works for your family). There are plenty of things they can choose that are free or very nearly free. Remind them of this. Compile a list of your local resources, from beach walks to local hills/mountains to be climbed and forest parklands to be explored. You could make a list and put them all into a jar and make it a lucky dip to choose which one you go to each week or simply compile a list and stick it up to cross off each one that you do. Equally, make it fun by taking photos, gathering up a small pebble/pine cone/leaf and so on from your time there and make a collage board/poster card when you get back.

Dance the moodies away: I strongly recommend this when the daily witching hour sets in (that hour with small children when you have played all there is to be played and read all of the books and yet there is still, somehow, an hour to go before bedtime and you have very little left to give... you know that hour; we *all* know that hour). Tensions are starting to run high, so dancing can work really nicely here as a way of getting more fun-based physical movement into your family routine. Play a song and for the duration of that song, everyone just dances, no commentary just movement, as whacky, wild and wily as you wish it to be or as coordinated as you choose. If this is your family's daily activity, try to make it last more than one song and let everyone choose a song each so that you can keep moving with very brief pauses in between (having a pre-compiled playlist for each of you will save time being lost while someone desperately searches for their song). At this stage of development you can also tweak this activity and invite your child to choose a song from an artist they really like and enjoy listening to. You can watch the music video for the song and either work together to learn and practise that routine (or make up your own version of it should it prove too complex) one step per day so that by the end of a week or so you have a nice routine you can move to in synchrony.

As detailed at the start of this book, our children's play patterns change at this stage of development and they become more drawn to screen-based play and sedentary activity so making the physical activities fun and interesting and exciting to engage with is crucial to bring them away from these screen-based devices. You have to find ways to make physical activity appealing and often this is enough to entice the most reluctant child to move away from the couch and do something with you.

Children who declare that they hate sports simply may not have found the type of physical activity that best suits them or that they can relate to. This is a case of *if they can't see it, they can't be it,* so again, watch and be mindful about how you relate to physical activity. If you are a super enthusiastic gym-bunny then perhaps your energy level is incongruent with theirs and you make it seem unattainable for them so they don't even try. Perhaps you also huff/puff/sigh and excuse not exercising and they are doing similar. Most likely, most of us fall somewhere in the middle and that is just about right. Don't we all remember what it was like to *have* to play some sport in school that we didn't enjoy at all (basketball for me, just not my thing and turned me off PE class for an entire term. Pause and think now – what's yours?)? Perhaps you can recall the relief and unexpected joy at finding an activity that really suited you, one that you quite looked forward to and were not tempted to find a reason to cancel the class (hot yoga for me. Pause and think now – what's yours?).

It can be reassuring to share these experiences with our kids and say it is okay to not like *this* sport but that doesn't mean you don't like *any* sport, we just haven't found *your* sport yet. Consider somewhat alternative sports or activities to the more traditional ones for this age group, such as baton twirling, fencing, rock climbing, biking, skateboarding, sea scouts, the scouts/girl guides, badminton, table tennis, boxing, yoga (for children) and many more. I know a child whose father managed to track down and enrol him in a juggling class as a way of getting him active and involved in something – and, believe me, there are more muscles involved in mastering juggling than you might think. Another parent I worked with spoke about how she loved to hula-hoop when she was her daughter's age but hadn't done it in years. Her daughter had never tried or really heard about hula-hooping so they bought two hula hoops and started to practise together. This mother laughed as she had utterly lost the knack of it in the years that had passed *but* what was lovely was that the joy it evoked in her was still alive and together they could (re)gain mastery over the task and in doing so together experience a shared joy.

Involving your child in the choice of activity can be empowering too. You can say that they must do something but they can choose between the three pre-approved activities (pre-approved for location, timing, affordability and so on) because if they choose it, they are more likely to do it. We are encouraging them to give it a go but it must be a decent commitment before they decide that they hate it and walk away, so if you have prepaid for a term of their chosen activity your expectation is that they see out the term but do not have to do a second if they really don't like it. This being said, do pay close attention to signs (both verbal and non-verbal) as to how they might be experiencing an activity and if they are showing signs of distress at the idea of participating, do stop and respond to this. In responding, you must simply accept that they do not like it, empathise with how this must feel and be curious as to what they specifically don't like about it to better understand their resistance.

Hold in mind that all-important question – is this fun? Make it fun to get it done!

THE WHAT IFFERY QUESTIONS...

I wanted to spend some time on this question because it is the one I hear so often. After I have listened and we have processed and worked through the presenting issue and perhaps, in a parenting context, I have dispensed some advice or suggestions. The parent I am speaking with will nod, pause to consider and then there is this moment, an inhale followed by, 'What if that doesn't work... What if I do all of that and the [bad thing] still happens?' The *what iffery*, as I call it, begins.

The reality is that bad news tends to engage our attention more than good and this leaves us predisposed to a negativity bias. Anyone who has a social-media account (most of us these days) and has ever posted something that garnered plenty of positive responses but also perhaps one or two negative responses knows first-hand what a negativity bias is because it is this default that causes us to dwell more readily on those two negative comments than on all of the positive ones around them. There is even neuroscientific evidence[5] to show that there is a higher degree of neural processing in the brain when processing negative stimuli. Anthropologically, our ancestors may have relied on this heightened alert around danger and negative stimuli to survive, their brains being primed for signs of threat and danger, meaning they could anticipate and be ready to respond to potentially life-threatening experiences. These days, while danger hasn't been eradicated from our lives, we certainly don't have the same need to be on constant alert, but we still tend to migrate towards a negativity bias in how we function and it has a significant impact on our lives in terms of our relationships (both intimate and platonic), how we perceive others and their intentions towards us and our decision-making capacity.

The good news, and you know that I will seek to positively reframe your negativity bias for you, is that there is research to show that our negative bias can actually serve as a motivational factor in terms of task completion. So when it comes to the *what iffery*, I want to greet it with a *Hi there, how are you? Come on in and stick the kettle on – let's get it said and learn from it*.

In order to achieve this, we have to be able to speak our negative bias out loud, so that we get to hear our own words, ideally share them with someone who can reflect back what they have heard us say and allow us to think deeper about the matter as we converse on it, and experience the reassurance that can come from being able to have an answer to those *what if* questions. If we know that we can speak our negative bias and use a positive reframing approach to work it through, we can change how it impacts us and how we relate to others around it. So let's do that now. I am going to ask and answer a series of *what ifs* based on the themes and topics we have already discussed and I'd like you to see if some of yours are covered here or if by reading these examples you can find your own path to positively reframing your own *what ifs*. Remember, if you can do this for yourself you are in a position to model how to do it with and for your child, thereby giving them a road map out of their negativity bias.

WHAT IF MY CHILD WILL NOT DO ANY CHORES?

The easiest way to have your 8–12-year-old agreeable or at least accepting of doing chores is to start them when they are very young and grow the responsibility up with them. I always say that part of being in a family is that everyone helps out, without being paid to do so. Children as young as two years old can start to participate in chores and help out. If this is not how you have approached it and are now trying to introduce an expectation of chores being done, you have to flag it as a change and a new expectation. All of you sit down together and explain that as your child is now older and able to take on more responsibility, you want them to be more responsible within your family home. Present two to three chores that they will be responsible for each week.

Anticipate some testing of this boundary – that is their job after all, and it is our job to hold those boundaries in a gentle yet firm, calm and consistent way. When you notice something hasn't been done, name it in a friendly calm reminder: 'I've noticed X isn't done. Remember that's your chore to do in our home. I'd really like you to take care of that as soon as possible.' If it still isn't done, move to an if/then approach: 'If you do the chores that are your responsibility, then I'll be able to take you to the park to meet your friends. If you don't do them, then I won't be able to take you.' If after this it still isn't done, hold your boundary and do not take them to meet their friends, saying, 'Thank you for letting me know that you don't want to be taken to meet your friends today,' and when they tell you how unfair you are, you simply reflect, 'You chose not to go meet your friends when you didn't do your chores. Tomorrow you get to make different choices about that.'

Boundaries are not about rigidity; they are gentle yet firm and flexible with the given child and situation. This is a really important age to start presenting opportunities for increased independence and personal responsibility. Chores and the above response are ways of upholding this system at this age and indeed into adolescence.

WHAT IF MY CHILD IS BULLIED?

This is another one that strikes at the very heart of any parent. We do not want to think about our child being hurt or scared by someone else, and we certainly don't want to think that they might be the ones who are hurting or scaring someone else.

Right now, I am inviting you to pause and take time to consider your child, not through *your* eyes but through the eyes of others. Be specific. Consider them through the eyes of their friends, their teacher, their sports coach and their relatives, and through the eyes of the child you know they don't get on with. I am not suggesting that if your child doesn't get on with another child it means they are bullying them, as it is perfectly okay to know that you are not compatible with some people and to limit your engagement, but you can and should still be respectful and kind in the engagement you do have with them. However, thinking about your child through the eyes of someone who doesn't really like them forces you to move out of your own biased perspective. It forces you to consider their less than desirable qualities or behaviour traits. We all have those too; indeed, this is an interesting exercise to do, applying it to yourself to reflect on how others might experience you. What have you learned about your child by doing this exercise? That they are not one dimensional – they are multi-faceted and have layers to their being? That, like anyone, your child will be triggered in response to certain situations and people and this will evoke or elicit an emotional response that will activate an overt behavioural action from them? This isn't about excusing anything that should not be excused, it is about shifting your perspective to truly *see* and *feel* your child from the inside out.

So, what if your child is bullied, in spite of you having invested in self-esteem and confidence building and raising an emotionally resilient child?

Bullying is about a need for power, more than the person being bullied per se, but the bully, in their quest for dominance over others/themselves/the group (perhaps all of these), will target someone they perceive as a threat to their dominance, who displaces them or whom they experience as problematic and not fitting what they deem to be the norm in others. Bullying is also extremely common in our children's social spheres, largely within school settings. We know that at this stage of development our children just want to be accepted, to fit in and to be included with their social group. It is precisely this tendency towards blending in with the clique that makes someone who doesn't, someone who stands out, vulnerable to being a target for bullying.

Quirks of personality, little traits or tendencies, the kinds of things that make your child who they are and who you love, are exactly the kinds of things that a bully will zone in on, amplify and seek to obliterate. And, of course, the answer is not to dull down the edges of your child in an attempt to make them blend in a bit more but to celebrate difference and diversity and to promote a culture of acceptance and empathy, of kindness, in our children. And you must ensure that your child has a clear plan in mind that they can default to if/when something like this might happen to them. This plan should be developed ahead of time, when there is no apparent need for it. It should be revisited and discussed and revised as they grow and develop, and it should hopefully be unused and never needed… but it is their *what if*.

- The plan should clearly define what bullying is and is not.
- The plan should clearly identify key steps to take that include:
  - Challenging the behaviour head-on: *Did you mean to come across as nasty as you did just there? I'm really uncomfortable with how you're behaving towards me and am asking you to stop now.*
  - Sharing and escalating: *Tell a friend straight away – never hold on to this feeling or keep the behaviour a secret. Tell two more people: your parent and your trusted teacher in school (or wherever it is happening).*
  - Asking 'what next?': *Discuss options openly: a) Seek to address it yourself; b) A parent comes with you to speak with the school/leader about this. If it is (a), know that*

the parent will check in with you and together review how it is going.

Making and discussing a plan of action at a time when the action is not needed allows you to really reflect on the topic in a calm way without heightened emotional arousal. Having such a plan also conveys a sense of control and confidence around a tricky topic.

Tip: We know that all of our schools are required to have a policy that deals with bullying so be sure to familiarise yourself with yours. In addition, be curious as to how your child's school upholds the policy ethos. A bullying or friendship awareness week once a year in school is nice but not as effective as the core ethos of acceptance and respect being an integral part of the school community on a daily basis. Have a think about ways you can suggest to your school to do this because there are endless ways to achieve it; below are just a few suggestions to get you started. Remember that our teachers are really busy so it is a kindness in and of itself to come to them with solutions rather than just the problems.

- **Hold daily class meetings:** The teacher could ask for reflections on local and world events, inviting children to share some of their emotional-/feeling-based news (inviting them to share isn't insisting that they share).
- **Have daily feeling check-ins:** Each classroom could have feeling expression masks/posters on a board and each day the children are invited to place a sticker on whichever feeling best describes them. The teacher can get a daily read on the mood in the room and build in appropriate group play or discussion to respond to this or check in with children who require it. This is also a great visual for all children to see that their peers have similar and also different feelings from them on different days.

- **Have a positive feelings mantra as a class motto each week:** This should be positively worded so rather than *Don't be mean to each other* it should state *We are kind to each other* or *We help each other* or *Everybody is important in our class*.

- **Build therapeutic stories into the class curriculum:** The teacher could have a set of books that have feelings at their core and in reading them to the class could invite the children to reflect on how a given character might feel about what happens. Do that character's feelings change over the course of the story and how/why does that change occur? What did they like about the story? The class is then separated into groups to come up with their own ending or their own drama point (the high point of the story) that they can draw and/or write out and share with the group.

- **Share lunch with a new friend:** The teacher could choose pairings in the classroom to ensure that children are paired with someone they might not typically play with or know very well. The children are asked to bring in something extra with their lunch that day and in their assigned pairs can share their food with each other and spend their lunchtime getting to know a peer a little better. After lunchtime, the class can share two new things they learned about their peer that they didn't know before.

- **Track, share and celebrate kindness:** Once a week, the children are invited to share an act of kindness they witnessed or actively engaged in. They can tell the story of the kind act and add in how it made them feel and how they think the other person(s) may have felt. This keeps them focused on observing, seeking and behaving in kind ways during their week so that they have something to share with the group. Remember and remind them that acts of kindness can be really small and don't need to involve cost or anything big.

- **Practise gratitude:** Have a weekly thank-you session. Each child is given a Post-it note to write a thank-you message for someone else in the class. Structure this to ensure everyone gives and receives a note by saying that they should keep it to the child they sit beside or let them pick a name out of a box and write one for that name. Again, remind them it might be for a kind smile that made them feel happy, being included in a game in the playground or the loan of a pencil.

- **Create group activities that reinforce connection in a positive way:** Have the class stand in a circle and the teacher starts by passing a non-verbal message around the group. For example, the teacher smiles at the child on their right and then that child turns and passes the smile to the next child and so on until it comes back to the teacher. Now reverse the direction and pass the smile the opposite way so that everyone in the group gives and receives from each other. Repeat this activity with a verbal message that is a compliment (about who you are not what you look like). The teacher passes 'I am happy to see you' or 'You are a kind person' and again reverses the direction once the compliment comes back to them.

BUT WHAT IF MY CHILD *IS* THE BULLY?

Imagine you receive that call from another parent to tell you that your child has been bullying theirs? What is your immediate reaction – I mean the first thought that comes into your head? How do you feel about that? Imagine being called into the school so that the headteacher can talk to you about your child's behaviour and the distress their actions have caused to another child. How does that feel? Is your instinct one of defensiveness and minimisation – 'Not my child, no way. This is being blown out of proportion!' Imagine going home to speak about this with your child – do

you know how you would approach this? This is what prompted
Lorcan's parents to come to see me.

*Lorcan was 10 years old when his parents came to see me. They
presented as mortified and humiliated and also really angry. It
was not immediately apparent whom this anger was directed
towards (Lorcan, themselves, the school, the other child in
question) but it was very present when I met with them that
first day. Mum described how she had received a call from the
school asking that she and Lorcan's dad attend for a meeting and
that it pertained to some behavioural issues involving Lorcan
and another child. I wondered what she had made of it in that
moment. She said she had assumed Lorcan had been in a fight
of some sort with another child and that she felt frustrated with
Lorcan but also that the school were overreacting: 'This is what
boys his age do – they get into fights, right?'*

*Then she described how they went to the school and were met
with the principal, vice-principal and the class teacher. 'When
I saw all of them there with such serious faces, my stomach
knotted and I thought "uh-oh, we're in trouble here".'*

*I wondered about this instinctual 'knowing' and her use of
'we' but at the time, she started to cry and Lorcan's dad picked
up the narrative. He spoke of how the principal quickly stated
the reason they were all there was that it had come to light
that Lorcan had been bullying another child in the class. The
teacher took over and explained that the parents of this other
child had spoken with her about it and how they had supervised
and observed Lorcan's behaviour for the next two weeks. She
confirmed that he was indeed bullying this child and not only
this child but also a number of his peers. She quickly cited
examples from a notebook in front of her with specific dates and
times that included targeted isolation, name-calling, physical
threats and actually being physical (this she clarified had been*

immediately broken up by a staff member when it was seen) and generally being nasty in his treatment towards and remarks about others. The vice-principal said that he had spoken with Lorcan about some of this behaviour as it occurred, talking to him about his language and name-calling and the fight in question, which he was clear Lorcan had instigated and involved Lorcan hitting another child rather than being fought with.

They were certain he was a bully and they were certain that their zero-tolerance policy would be invoked, meaning that Lorcan was to be immediately suspended pending a full hearing. They had strongly advised that his parents seek psychotherapeutic intervention for him in this time both because he needed it (they felt) and also as a clear sign that they were taking the matter seriously when it would come to the hearing with the school board.

I reflected what I had heard and made some clarifications and then added, 'I haven't heard you mention anything that you said at this meeting.' Mum said she had cried ('just like I am now'), and Dad said, 'This was a meeting with an outcome already decided and we were just being told about it.' And so they were here with me.

I wondered how Lorcan had reacted. They said that he had initially denied it, then minimised it and then sought to blame others before becoming angry. Denial (I didn't do it), minimisation (it isn't a big deal anyway), blame (it's YOUR fault that this happened, not mine) and rage (projected outward at someone else so I might go on the attack, or inwards on myself whereby I might shut down or hurt myself) all point to shame-based behaviours. Shame is an uncomfortable feeling, difficult to contain, so shame-based people will use these associated defensive strategies to try to manage that extreme discomfort inside themselves. I wondered about Lorcan outside this, how he had been as a very young child and how he had negotiated the world and the people in it as he grew up. I also asked about any significant life events that Lorcan had had to deal with in his life to date. This wasn't an attempt to excuse his behaviour but rather to explain and even better understand it.

His parents gave me a generalised developmental history, that he had been a very lovely baby and easy to parent for the first couple of years. They described him as being very difficult around toddlerhood, especially from two-and-a-half to four years old when his 'terrible twos' just seemed endless and he became very hard to manage. We explored discipline at this stage and they said they had used a number of behaviour modification methods as seen on parenting TV shows (sticker charts, time-outs, etc.). The problem with these measures is two-fold for me. Lorcan was not developmentally old enough to avail of either option and both contain a level of shaming for the child who isn't able to really understand them. A sticker chart is something that hangs in the house (in their kitchen in this instance) for anyone who calls to see it and can know that he is in trouble – that is shaming. Another challenge with the sticker chart is that it can, inadvertently and particularly for the shame-based child, reinforce a belief that only perfection is acceptable in terms of behaviour. (**Note: Of course you can modify this method to be more reflective and accepting but this was not the case here – generally there are options other than behaviour charts that can be considered.**)

The time-out calls for a child to sit in isolation, reflect on their negative behaviour and, after a set time determined by the adult, show their reflection and make repair. Now bear in mind that children under seven years old don't self-regulate their emotional states; they co-regulate with their caregivers and parents. So sitting on a step or in a time-out at three years old is futile. He couldn't have done what was expected of him, and sitting there only separated him from his secure base and left him to fester in rage and shame waiting to be invited back in with that magic word 'sorry'. I do not reflect this to infer that this alone can account for his behaviour because Lorcan must and should be held accountable for his behaviour and the choices he made; nor am I saying his parents did this to him, because they didn't. However, Lorcan did not integrate or experience 'correction within connection' and did not have parents who helped to make sense of his behaviour as underpinned by emotional and physical states and reflect this back to him in a way that enabled growth and learning (about himself, others and the world around him, i.e. he was not supported in the development of his emerging sense of self).

When I met with Lorcan he was angry and defensive far more than he was contrite or remorseful. He felt exposed, vulnerable and shamed by what had happened and felt his parents no longer would love him because 'I'm a bad person'. I simply acknowledged his fears and added, 'You did a bad thing but you're NOT a bad person, Lorcan.' He didn't understand the difference and this marked the start of our work.

We worked together for six months, weekly, and I felt as if I got to see Lorcan in all of his parts – his anger that was first to greet me but also his fear, his confusion, his hurt, his sharp wit and engaging sense of humour, his generosity, his reflective self, his joy and his kindness. Our focus was on building acceptance and empathy both within and around/towards Lorcan so I also involved his parents in a block of these sessions and met with them for psycho-education support around how to best support Lorcan emotionally and behaviourally.

I worked with Lorcan on the understanding that I would confirm to the school that he was actively attending sessions with me but not that I would write a letter in support of him staying in school or seek to explain away his actions. I wanted

Lorcan to choose to see me for his own benefit and not for the secondary gain of me lobbying the school to keep him in. I felt and still feel strongly that Lorcan would draw long-term and meaningful benefit from our work on these terms and that he should face the consequences of his behaviour and actions whatever that might be. I could also see that behind the anger Lorcan could see the pain he had caused others. He reflected that he 'knew' the other kids didn't really like him and so he became the kid not to like and he hated it and it made him angry and ashamed and so he spilled that rage and shame outwards (because it is so hard to contain) onto others until he really did become the kid no one liked.

At his school's disciplinary hearing, Lorcan apologised to the children in question and their parents, and he meant it. He said that he did bully the others and he felt ashamed and wanted to change how he behaved. His school committee (made up of staff, board of management and importantly two pupils) decided that he would serve a two-week suspension with schoolwork sent home and that he would then return to school and also that he would have to volunteer on the school's anti-bullying committee and help organise their friendship week. This last bit was a suggestion of the two pupils on the committee and was the part that Lorcan really responded to, initially with anxiety and resistance because he didn't know how to make a connection with his peers in a positive way. However it was an experience he grew to appreciate and then really enjoy, and he flourished in this role and became an active and engaged pupil in the school community, with friends.

I share this example with you to highlight that **repair following a rupture** like discovering your child *is* the bully is absolutely possible and also that there is valuable learning in facing up to our actions, taking accountability and accepting the consequences of these actions. I believe that Lorcan acknowledging his behaviour, apologising and seeking to make repair through change and working hard on himself were key aspects of making a meaningful and long-term change. However, it was also necessary to give his parents that space in psycho-education sessions to process their own anger and disappointment. This allowed them to reflect on how this Lorcan wasn't who they thought he was and how sad they felt that he had managed to conceal so much of himself from them without them seeing it. They had to relearn their son, to love and accept him for who he really was and to step up and in towards him to take their role in his journey forward and out of this place.

WHAT IF MY CHILD STEALS?

This is another tricky one as the developmental task of risk-taking behaviour mixed with the peer influence, group or herd mentality effect (as they conform to group thinking to feel accepted or fit in), and the thrill of 'being bad' and trying to get away with something (and the associated adrenalin rush in the process) is attractive to your middle-childhood-staged child, most especially at that upper age of pre-teen. I am referring to the fairly typical stealing behaviour we can see emerge at this stage of development rather than a more serious, pervasive behaviour that would reach the threshold for a diagnosis of kleptomania. This is a psychological condition where the person is experiencing a compulsion to steal rather than being motivated in the moment to take something of material or financial value to them. A kleptomaniac cannot resist the urge to steal, and the stealing is generally spontaneous rather than pre-planned and tends to (not always) take place in public places like shops. Kleptomania is a psychological condition that requires the clinical intervention of a suitably trained and qualified professional.

This is not what I am writing about here. I am referring to a more developmentally typical type of stealing and associated lying that corresponds with a child's stage of development. It is something they can control and has (usually) been planned and built up to and may (not always but often at this stage) take place in collaboration with peers, as in the child steals *with* a friend or friends.

Under nine years old (sometimes even 10 years old depending on your child's emotional maturity, and remember I mean developmental age rather than chronological) your child may not have developed a meaningful understanding of moral judgement or how the rules in society work. Even if they show some grasp of this, they can be easily swayed into seeing them as they apply to others rather than themselves or will be motivated to try to get around the rules and think they will simply get away with the behaviour. However, we do expect that by the age of nine children will have developed a sense of appreciation and respect for what belongs to others and fully understand that it is not theirs to simply take. They will generally understand, by this age, that there will be consequences for taking what doesn't belong to them and, in line with their pronounced sense of justice and fairness, will grasp how they would feel if someone took something that belonged to them.

As stated above, the pressure to be accepted by their peer group or perhaps significant self-esteem issues can motivate this type of behaviour. Just as you may see stealing at this age, you may also observe that it is accompanied by lying as they attempt to deny responsibility and project it away from themselves. Perhaps they don't want to get anyone else in trouble or perhaps they are ashamed of what they have done and are struggling to own the behaviour and address/accept your disapproval and disappointment in them.

One of the reasons this is such a trigger for parents is that it can happen outside home and therefore involve other people. Once discovered, it can be very difficult to contain the behaviour within your own family or even parent–child relationship. It is worth pausing and considering why you might want to keep this behaviour a secret. Is it because it reflects badly on your child? On you? Both? Either way it is largely because it is a shameful behaviour and even though it can be more common at this age than you would think it to be, it is still not an acceptable or healthy behaviour and it does need to be responded to in the right way.

You can drill into them your sense of moral right/wrong, teach them the value of money by assigning chores and insisting they save some of their pocket money and work up towards buying a treat for themselves and then one day you get a call to say your child has been caught shoplifting or you discover that they have been stealing from your handbag or wallet.

The parental instinct is to quickly move to confront and punish the behaviour, place the child on some kind of restriction (grounded, no screen devices, no pocket money) and perhaps start hiding where your wallet is in the house or not allowing them to enter a shop without you present. But does this address or even seek to better understand the behaviour and the impulse behind it? I'm not saying you should condone it – perhaps the above punishments are indeed warranted – but it shouldn't be at a cost of developing deeper understanding into this behaviour through your child's eyes.

We know, as adults, that the stuff we want must be worked hard for and earned. We know that stealing from a shop affects the staff and owner of that shop. Do not assume your child truly 'gets' this, however, because in their world this isn't how it works or really has ever worked thus far. When they want something they ask the adult in charge to get it for them. Perhaps we say yes/no or not now but we, the adult in charge, gets to decide this. In this way we are the people in power who can give and take away things that children want to have. Yes, we can teach them to save up and work towards something, but even when they buy the lip gloss or starter make-up set or video game they have desired and worked hard to earn money for, *we* still get to say when that make-up can be worn and when that game can be played – we still hold power. I'm not suggesting you change this. I am simply suggesting we pause and consider it from our children's point of view to gain a deeper understanding of why on earth they would do something like *steal*.

This is an age of seeking more independence and, of course, power in their own lives. They want to establish a stronger sense of self and will experiment from now on (this ups a notch in the teen years, so brace yourself) with rules and risk – and isn't stealing the perfect way to do just that, with a little high adrenalin thrill thrown in?

When they are 'found out' there will likely, for most children, be a strong sense of embarrassment, shame and regret. What is vital is that you stay in the moment. It is not that they are a thief, never to be trusted around money or shops again. They have made a choice to steal on this occasion, but you may not know if this is the first time or not. What you are focused on is that it becomes the last time. I would dissuade anyone from concealing their wallet or purse at this age but be very clear that there is trust and transparency in your family. You will be leaving your bag wherever it always is and you expect no one to steal from it. If your child steals you must address it head-on.

- Be certain they did steal from you or a shop (no assumptions but have evidence to support your claim).
- Express your feeling in response to this behaviour – disappointment, anger, sadness and frustration.
- Invite them to own up and own the behaviour.
- If they don't take responsibility, offer a modified consequence system – *If you don't discuss this with me your consequence is twice what it would be if you did discuss it with me.*

Most children will choose a lesser consequence; they have been caught anyway and you need to get them talking *with* you about this rather than you simply preaching *at* them. Remember, *correction within a connection* is most effective in changing behaviour in a meaningful and sustained way.

Your child is still the same child you had before you discovered this behaviour, and they have simply made a bad choice rather than become a bad child so do not respond to them as though *they* are bad. Children steal for many different reasons:

- It's exciting and thrilling in this time of risk-taking behaviour.
- They want to impress or seem cool and thereby be accepted by a peer group.
- They feel pressured into it by a peer group.
- They want to test the rules and limits on behaviour (parental and societal).
- They have other more significant issues.

For this last point, we need to look at the bigger picture to assess if the stealing is simply part of a pattern of troublesome behaviours; if the child in question shows regret or remorse at their actions when caught; if this is an on-off/infrequent behaviour or something they do or have done a lot of. In this case, it is important to seek consultation from child and adolescent mental-health services to explore and respond to any other issues around the stealing.

Very often, stealing goes hand in hand with those other charming behaviours, lying and cheating. In the same vein as stealing, mild to moderate degrees of lying and cheating tend to be a feature of this stage of development and will appear in varying levels in various children. Not even your own children will all display these traits in the same way; some children barely dip a toe in lying and cheating and would never try stealing, whereas others will give all three a fairly good go during these years. A simple yet effective game to play around these themes is **Spot the lie**.

15-minute play tip

Spot the lie, or as I sometimes call it **Truths and lies**, is a game where each participant tells three pieces of information, two of which must be truths and one a lie. It is up to the other participants to spot the lie. It can be fun to share afterwards how you could tell which one was the lie or what led you to make that guess. Try to be creative with the lies and even the truths you share. It shouldn't be *too* obvious which one is the lie; there should be cause to pause, read the non-verbal cues of the other person and make a guess.

One way to parent against the lure of such rule-breaking and the limit-testing behaviours detailed above is to shine a spotlight (early and often as they continue to grow and develop) on the truth. Make telling the truth appealing and something you welcome and work with them around, even if that truth is to share some negative action, because in telling you the truth now they are able to take some responsibility for the behaviour and you can work with that.

DEALING WITH RESISTANCE

You know how it goes: no matter what you seem to suggest it is met with a shrug of disinterest, an eye-roll or an outright 'no'. Resistance is a phase of development that spans the entire spectrum of childhood, appearing in slightly different guises as your child continues to grow and develop.

Resistance is itself a thing to be aware of. There are different kinds of resistance and understanding what kind you are seeing will be very helpful in informing your responses and ultimately guiding your child through it. When something is new it is not unusual that it is met with an initial positive response, like a so-called honeymoon phase. This is a phase of excited exploration – they are curious, it is new and it is engaging. Following this explorative phase we can be met with resistance. *I've dipped my toe in, I have a sense of it all and I've decided to pull back.* But why? This is the crucial bit. Is it what we might call a neurological resistance, as in does your child have a neurological developmental challenge that renders the activity beyond their capacity or accounts for their emotional withdrawal? Or is this a resistance that is presented as an *I don't like it; it's boring* when actually it might be too challenging, too intense, a little overwhelming? If the latter is the case, your child may need your support in talking to the instructor or coach to modify the task for them, or simply some time and support from you to help them work their way through it.

If you can help them to work through the resistance, it generally leads them to a tentative acceptance of the rules, set-up and the personalities involved, and then they are fully engaged and connected to the activity/group/club. So when you are met with resistance from your child (useful beyond this topic of physical activity resistance), start by determining the underlying cause of the behaviour you are seeing, and so long as there is no emotional trauma or neurological basis to the resistant behaviour, you can explore it as a typical resistance or perhaps a specific resistance to a person or aspect of the activity (perhaps they really cannot work with the coach/instructor or there is an issue with the group dynamic that is making them resist the activity).

Resistance or lack of cooperation is a signal of discomfort or distress. By staying curious and seeking to better understand what is happening from your child's point of view you will avoid a defensive response (i.e. you insist or demand they go and are met with total shut down). This will deepen your understanding and empathic awareness of your child's experience, which you can then reflect back to them in understanding, acceptance and empathy, enabling them to better understand what has happened for themselves. This doesn't mean you simply say, 'Oh, you don't like it, that's okay, don't go anymore,' because if it is a more typical resistance, one that is in the mild to moderate range, the best response is to gently yet firmly challenge your child's negative view of themselves and engage them in spite of mild discomfort so that they learn how to tolerate mild tension-arousing experiences and draw benefit from gaining mastery over a task. This more mild to moderate or less serious level of discomfort can arise when a child has limited experience of having to cooperate or interact with new people outside their typical (school) peer group, or indeed groups in general if they are new to group or team activity. In this way, such resistance to the activity may indicate low confidence, fear of failure and discomfort in having to abide by the group rules rather than being able to do it their own way. Learning to overcome and negotiate through these feelings are important life skills at this stage of development.

All of this being said, do be reasonable and fair in what you are expecting of them. Factor in their stage of development when encouraging them to choose an activity. At this stage of middle childhood most (typically developing) children can engage in more complex sports such as volleyball, basketball, cricket, hockey, rugby, football and so on because they have generally developed good enough hand-eye coordination, motor skills and a grasp of rules (this is also why team sports can be so appealing at this age).

Also bear in mind that physical activity does not have to equal sport as detailed in the examples and suggested activities above. Just finding ways to get moving while having a laugh is a great start... it doesn't always have to be heart-pumping, sweat-inducing activities.

Remember that *encouraging* is not *insisting* or *demanding* and the experience will bring the greatest benefit when you focus on and praise the effort rather than the outcome. Avoid pressuring your child into doing something (it will only elicit greater resistance) and never use physical activity as a reward or punishment to incentivise behaviour. It should simply be something that you do as part of your healthy family routine and lifestyle.

INVEST IN MINDFUL COMMUNICATION

In general, the type of communication that helps to strengthen and enhance the parent–child relationship (at this stage of development and beyond) and also serves to model good emotional self-regulation skills, which are key life skills at this age, is what I would refer to as conscious or *mindful communication,* whereby you seek to:

- invite a contribution from your child on all topics
- be curious about them, their lives, their friends, their thoughts, feelings and experiences – *all of them*
- notice and name their good intentions, regardless of outcome
- always be open to connection with them
- acknowledge their feelings about something, whether or not you agree
- invite cooperative solutions to problems that arise in your relationship with them by asking them what they would do in the situation: 'If YOU were the parent, what would you do in this situation?'
- stay out of judgement when naming the behaviours or actions you are displeased with
- follow up on things you have been talking about and set a time to do so. Remember this time and check in with them to see if they want to revisit the discussion because in

simply doing that, even if they turn you down, they notice that you remembered and held them in mind

- set attainable goals in what you are asking of them – be realistic and developmentally appropriate, manage your expectations and don't set them up to fail by aiming too high, too fast
- use non-verbal as much as verbal cues – focus on *doing* your communication as opposed to just *speaking* it
- validate and accept their needs, thoughts and feelings
- when in doubt, go to A&E – *acceptance and empathy.*

Take 15 minutes and have fun with it by trying out this communication activity. You will need three of you or more. One person is the runner and two are builders, identified as A and B (if you have more they are observers and get to step in and have a go when this round is done). The two builders are each given a set of identical building blocks and stand away from each other, with their backs turned to each other so they cannot see what the other is doing. Person A builds a structure, the runner looks at them doing this and goes back over to person B and tells them how to build the structure based on what they have observed. At the end, the aim is that both structures will be identical based on the good communication of the runner.

Another fun one that reinforces the skill of reading non-verbal communication is the **sit down game.** There are two ways to do this and it works best if you have a family or group of more than four people. Set a rule that two people must be standing at any one time but *only* two people. These two people can only stand for 20 seconds at a time. So if Mum and eldest child are standing, within 20 seconds they must sit down (not at same time necessarily) and as they move to do so the others must anticipate their action before they sit so that two people are always standing. Another way to do this is to have everyone stand in a circle and nominate a leader for each round. The group stands in silence and watches the leader for when they start to sit as the whole group must sit down at the exact same time. If anyone is out of sync they all get back up and wait and try again.

Describe and draw is a fun game to play that supports communication too. Take two chairs and place them so that two people are seated back to back. One is identified as A and one as B. A is handed an object by another person or simply picks an object themselves and must verbally describe that object without naming what it is. B must draw the object based on A's description and see if the object can be matched/identified at the end.

Play is a great and very effective interactive way to support your child's evolving communication skills. It is also a great way to strengthen and enhance your own communication with your child(ren) in a way that is positive, fun and laughter based.

CHAPTER 8

Some Notes for Parents of Children with Special Needs when Planning Play Activities

Play is important for all children. In the past, the perception has been that children with disabilities, special needs and especially children with cognitive delay are not interested in play. This is not the case and it is vital that you take time to learn your child's capacity for playful engagement, trial what works and use play as a means of communicating with them. Play is the universal language of all children, regardless of ability.

Parents play an important role in facilitating play for children with special and/or additional needs. You need to be aware of the challenges faced by your child and know how to adapt the environment and encourage your child to explore the possibilities for play. You must also ensure that your child with special needs has opportunities to self-initiate play, even though adult modelling of play may be required before your child is able to play independently.

Siblings and other children without special needs might be helpful 'play partners' when they have some understanding that their sibling/friend has some special needs that mean they play a little differently to other children.

When it comes to assessing or choosing suitable play activities for your child with special needs, bear in mind that children can display more advanced skill development in play activities than in clinical testing. The best way to work out what play will suit your child is by trying a range of activities and seeing what works best. Props (toys) can be handy and even helpful in playing with your child but remember that *you* are the best play prop (toy) your child will ever have. So get comfortable coming down to their level, engage with your playful self and have fun together. Games like **Row, row, row your boat** or **thumb wrestling** or **hand-stacking** or **holding/rocking** do not require any props other than you.

The environment plays an important role in accessibility to play for children with special needs. The indoor environment needs to be modified to accommodate children with different capabilities and ranges of motion. Especially important are modifications of space and accessible location of materials for children using wheelchairs and other mobility aids.

Remember, *you* are the expert on your child, and no one will ever know them in the way that you do. Trust your instincts, safely push through some perceived limits to explore the range of play your child is capable of and discover what gives them pleasure and enjoyment because that's what play is about. When children are having fun their cortisol levels or stress hormones lower, they are more relaxed and they learn/retain more from what they are doing. As a result, they grow and develop, and that is what children are really about – growing and developing as people.

15-minute play ideas that meet your child's unique and/or additional needs

This is a long list of play simply because no two children who live with special needs are the same in their development and as such only some of what I am including here will be applicable to you and your child. Equally, there may be something in this list that won't work exactly with your child but might inspire you to modify it so that it would.

Sensory tables: These offer a wealth of benefits for children with special needs. Engaging in sensory experiences like running fingers through dried rice or pouring water can distract and calm a child who is feeling over-stimulated or anxious. It promotes self-discovery and encourages a child to explore new textures, which in turn supports social and emotional development.

Offering textures like dried beans, sand or cotton balls promotes hand-eye coordination and gives the opportunity for a child to pinch and grasp, enhancing fine motor skills. As children discover new textures and objects, they tend to have a verbal response. Engaging them in a sensory table is great way to work on language development.

Sensory basins: For a *wet sensory basin,* half fill a bowl with warm (not hot) water. Add a squirt of washing-up liquid (don't mix just add it in). Add in a teaspoon of cinnamon or ginger. Add a handful of glitter (diamond glitter is best in water). Give your child a hand-held whisk and allow them to stir the water. This will form bubbles while they see the glitter sparkle and smell the cinnamon/ginger, giving them significant sensory stimulation. Depending on your child's capacity you can take a straw each and when you say 'green light' everyone blows into the water, making bubbles grow bigger and bigger. When you say 'red light' everyone stops blowing and pops the bubbles with their straw or their finger. Your child might also like to put some small toys into the basin and play in the water.

For a *dry sensory basin,* fill a bowl/basin with (uncooked) red and green lentils, add in some (uncooked) bow-tie-shaped pasta because it looks like butterflies. Get two small cups/flower pots (the tiny seed-planting size) and have your child run their hands through the contents of the bowl, pour from one cup into the other and you may even bury something in the bowl so that they must burrow through with their hands to find it.

Outdoor play: This is stimulating for children of all abilities and specifically those who need a little extra help developing gross motor skills. When engaging children in outdoor playtime, organise specific games like kicking or passing a ball between you or hopscotch, **Simon Says**, **Mother May I** and **Red Light, Green Light** (where the child can go/move at green light and must stop when you say red light – note that you can do this either directing whole-body movement such as hop when you say green light or something much smaller if more appropriate for your child, like wiggle your fingers or stamp your foot when you say green light). Games like these promote whole-body movement and balance while teaching children to follow directions and focus their attention. Also good are **Head, Shoulders, Knees and Toes** and **The Hokey-Cokey** and singing **If You're Happy and You Know It** clap your hands/wiggle your fingers/stamp your feet/shake your head.

Offering plenty of options for *free play* is important too. When given pavement chalk and outdoor equipment like balls and hula hoops, children will engage their fine and gross motor skills without even realising it.

Yoga: Children of all abilities can benefit significantly from yoga, a practice that balances the mind and body. With practice, children who have a hard time sitting still can learn to self-regulate physically and emotionally and self-soothe using movement and breathe to calm themselves. It helps to build self-awareness of the body and a variety of emotional states. Many yoga poses are named after animals, so it's easy to incorporate stories with the poses and make the practice fun. Children can *slither like snakes* or *roar like fierce lions*, all while learning how to focus in a pose. Here is an example:

Frog pose

- Squat on the floor, balancing on your toes with knees spread wide apart. Place hands on the floor between your legs.
- Look up and inhale.
- As you exhale, straighten your legs and lower your head towards your knees.
- Return to squatting position and repeat.

A light box: This is fun and visually very appealing for all children, but it specifically helps to increase the attention spans and the capacity for prolonged engagement of children with special needs. Children can spend hours with a light box, exercising their fine motor skills by creating illuminated patterns and pictures with brightly coloured transparent shapes. Even better, this easy home-made version works great at home. Be sure to have plenty of brightly coloured transparent items on hand like decorating rocks, plastic blocks and even coloured salt.

You will need: one large clear plastic storage tub, two strings of fairy lights, some large sheets of tracing paper (plain or coloured) and sellotape. To assemble the light box, line the inside of the tub lid with tracing paper and secure with tape. This will help create an even distribution of light. Drill a small hole in the corner of the tub and feed the string of lights through. Arrange them evenly on the bottom of the tub. Place the lid on top of the tub and plug in the lights.

Music (activities based on rhythm and synchrony): Music activates every subsystem in the brain, including areas that regulate emotion and motivation. Setting aside specific time to sit and make music together allows children to bond with family members and gives them a sense of containment.

Music time can be especially beneficial to children who are non-verbal. For them, music can be a way of expressing themselves and interacting with their peers. Provide children with instruments, like egg shakers, bells or toy drums. You can make your own instruments, for example by pouring dried peas into an empty Pringles tube and sellotaping the lid on (decorate the tube or wrap it in colourful paper) to make a shaker; equally, using an empty baby formula food container with a burst balloon stretched over the open top and secured in place will make a great finger drum. Encourage the children to make noise with their instruments and move their bodies to the music. Sing songs that incorporate the name of each child so that everyone feels that they have an individual role in the activity, for example, 'James is here today, James is here today, clap our hands and shout hooray that James is here today' and repeat for everyone's name – even if there are just two of you doing it.

Additionally, incorporate music in other activities of the day. Sing songs while cleaning up and transitioning into new activities like nap or snack time: 'We are cleaning up our toys, we are cleaning up our toys, it's fun to sing and make some noise while cleaning up our toys' or something like this to the tune of your choosing.

Your child will be better able to do some of these than others, especially at first, so use your parental instinct in selecting appropriate tasks.

Sand play/Play-Doh/finger painting/water play: These are also good sensory experiences for young children. Allow them time alone playing this as well as joining them in this play.

Use your tone of voice to mirror how they are playing: For example, in a high-pitched voice and at a very fast pace say, 'Oh my goodness that car is going really really fast' or in a low, quieter, more monotone voice say, 'Oh no, you threw that toy across the room because you're feeling sad and angry' (this doesn't mean they shouldn't have to pick it back up – they should!). By helping them to hear their feelings in your tone they will be better able to integrate them.

Clay modelling: Crayola Model Magic (or similar product) is a softer and cleaner form of clay that little fingers find more malleable and they can build things, let them go hard and paint them and then see them on a shelf at home.

Lullaby: Have your child curl up on your knee and ensure eye contact between you and them, wrapping them up in a soft blanket. You sing a lullaby to the tune of 'Twinkle, Twinkle Little Star' but using words particular to the child, such as 'Twinkle, twinkle little star, what a special girl you are. Long brown hair and soft pink cheeks. Big brown eyes from which you peek. Twinkle, twinkle little star, what a special girl you are!' (Edit words as you see fit, as appropriate to your child.)

Pop cheeks: Fill your own cheeks with air and gently guide your child's hands to push gently on your cheeks with their fingers so that the air pops out. Then encourage them to do the same and you pop their cheeks.

Hand-stack: Put lotion on your hands and your child's hands and make a hand-stack, alternating each of your slippy hands, moving from bottom to top each time.

Various experiences with touch and textures: Experiment with lotioning, making hand or foot prints in powder, pressing hands or feet into Play-Doh or shaving cream, using baby oil for back rub with the child facing you, face painting, finger painting. Be aware of possible sensitivities to odours and amend accordingly.

Activities promoting eye contact: Put a sticker on your nose and help your child pull it off; put a cotton ball on your nose with a dab of lotion and let the child blow it off. Blow bubbles in front of the child and help them pop the bubbles with their fingers or toes.

CHAPTER 9

Preparing for the Next Stage

The core messages of this book have been about spotlighting the importance of this most under-discussed stage of childhood, the middle-childhood years. I have always found this stage of childhood clinically fascinating. It is a time of huge growth and development and brings with it a myriad of mixed emotions, both for the child and the parent. Your child is starting to pull away from you but only so that they can initiate the process of separation and individuation that sets them up for adolescent development. They will be more drawn to their peer group and perhaps to forming new friendships with children very different from you and yours that enable them to separate further from you. It is a stage of increased focus on justice and fairness, mostly as it relates to them but also a time for them to become really interested and even passionate about social causes that resonate with them.

What matters most at this stage is that you keep play alive in your relationship with your child. Their play patterns and styles and preferences will begin to change now, with increased focus on group play like team sports and structured activity play such as trampolining, scooters, bikes, and less imaginative play than you will have seen in earlier childhood. So we have to stay playful, curious and engaged with them and their lives (remember, though, interested is not intrusive) and, above all, accepting and empathic about how they see the world at this time.

This stage of childhood is about priming your relationship for the adolescent years, and good solid investment now will stand you in good stead as they move into these years. This is also a great time to check in with yourself and ensure that you are *growing your parenting up* in line with your child's development. It is the perfect time to start Teflon-coating yourself (so to speak) to de-personalise the rejection and conflict ahead. It is in this stage of development that the same child who begged you to chaperone their school trips on every school tour now wants you to walk on the opposite side of the road to them when you are out. They have moved from being so proud to show you off to being embarrassed by how you look, how you dress, how you sound (that's literally the sound of your voice never mind what you are saying) and it is really difficult not to take that personally. But while it is personal, it is actually not personal to you. These attacks on you are really a projection of their own increased self-consciousness and embarrassment as they try to wriggle out of early childhood into and then through this middle-childhood phase.

Stay away from me; you're so embarrassing = I feel overwhelmed and can't make sense of my feelings right now so it's easier for me to push you away than try to work this out.

Just as they did in toddlerhood, your children now need you to help them to make sense of the feelings they are experiencing and develop a deeper understanding of how those feelings are what underpin and inform their (less than pleasant) overt behaviours. That is the job of this stage and, again as you did in toddlerhood, keeping the relationship playfully connected with gentle yet firm boundaries is what will get you through this.

I'm sorry you're having a hard time right now. I do hear that you need some space so let's get this task done and then you can have an uninterrupted hour alone before dinnertime, okay? (And if this isn't enough) Okay, I can see this isn't going to happen right now, so take the time alone and we can think about doing this at another time when it's easier for you to be around me.

This is a good time to create some stock replies that you can reach for in those tricky moments when you actually may feel like losing it. Having three to five generalised responses is a good idea. For example:

- *You have strong feelings about this and I understand your reasons why but I need some time to think it through. Let's discuss it again later on after dinner.*
- *I think you've forgotten how we speak to each other in this family. Would you like to try that again or take short a break until you can?*
- *I can feel myself getting really angry and irritated with how this conversation is going and I don't want to lose my temper with you so I need to walk away for 15 minutes alone before we continue.*
- *I know that you don't always understand my reasons for saying no or stopping you from doing something and it might not always feel fair to you, but part of my job as your parent is to make tough decisions that keep you safe. This is one of those times and my decision isn't going to change.*
- *We have different views on this and that's okay; everyone won't always agree with you and that can be really frustrating. What do you need to do to calm down? Can I help you with that?*

These types of responses fit within *acceptance* (accepting that how they feel right now is valid and true to what is happening for them) and *empathy* (you can convey a *felt understanding* that their struggle is real and of them, not you), and memorising them so that you can recite them easily in those more contentious moments will be a great shield to protect your parental self in this phase of middle childhood.

And, of course, all of this is to get you both ready to embark on the rocky and risky road of adolescence. For now, it will be enough to seek to stay in the moment with where you and your child are at right now, trusting that you are working towards a new phase but not trying to project too far into the future.

As your child reaches the end of the period from eight to 12 years, set yourself a few goals to prepare for the next stage of parenting:

- Always encourage them to play, whatever that looks like for your child now and remember that experimenting with music, opinions, clothes and make-up *is* play.
- Encourage imaginative and creative thinking; it helps them work out solutions to problems they will encounter as they grow. Do this by *wondering* about the things they say or the things you hear when you are together.
- Identify opportunities to encourage and support them to practise consistent types of independence as this will help them assert themselves in a confident yet respectful way with others. Make sure that you encourage them to interact with service staff in restaurants or sales staff in shops to ask for what they want.
- When something doesn't work out as they wanted it to, sit with them *in* their disappointment but don't rescue them from it. Rather, support them in finding their way out of it with fresh thinking and a new perspective.
- Give them areas of their life (including at home with you) when they can show leadership, and always praise their efforts over outcomes.
- They will still need you and depend on you a lot, so be as available as you can be, but it is vital that your parenting

grows up as they do. Trust your children and trust that you have been – and continue to be – good enough.

This is a stage of parenting where we really experience the push/pull of attachment evolution. The more we seek to pull them towards us, the more they seem to push us away. It can feel as if you are damned if you do and damned if you don't, but hold on tight, this is a phase of their evolving childhood. They are not supposed to be making you feel good about yourself or even that you are a good parent – that just isn't their responsibility (at any stage of parenting) – but if you stay rooted and trust the process, trust your parenting instincts and trust your love and relational bonds, this too shall pass. The important thing is that you do not allow them to push you too far away but you stand your ground, gentle yet firm, and accept that they will push against you but you know what to do and that they still have to lean into you. Take that – that's enough right now.

And it is certainly not all doom and gloom because there are chinks in this armour they are trying out. The joyful moments of meeting are still there and available to you and it is so important that you do avail of these. Keeping play an active part of your parent–child relationship now helps you to spotlight those cracks and even expand and grow them.

Build yourself a jar of joy for when the wheels do come off… and some days they will, but that is okay too. For your **positivity jar**, take a jar (optimistically, make it a large one) and a stack of coloured notes. When there are those lovely joyful moments of meeting, when you experience that shared joy together with your child, write it down on one of your coloured notes, fold it up and pop it in your jar. Keep doing this, and there truly will be plenty of opportunity to fill your jar. This is not a time-sensitive project – it is open-ended and you can keep filling it up. Visually you will have a jar filled with brightly coloured folded notes, which will look nice but also even at a glance serve to remind you of all the lovely moments you have had in your relationship with your middle-childhood child/pre-teen. On particularly trying days, reach in, pick one out and read it to yourself to bring you back to the shared joy in your relationship. This will help to stop you spiralling down when you have a bad day or even a bad couple of days.

A LETTER FROM JOANNA

I want to say a huge thank you for choosing to read my 15-Minute Parenting series. If you did enjoy it, and want to keep up to date with all my latest releases, just sign up at the following link. Your email address will never be shared and you can unsubscribe at any time.

www.thread-books.com/joanna-fortune

Why 15 minutes? is the most common question I get asked about this book series and my answer is this: in my clinical practice with families, the most common thing I heard from time-poor parents is that after finishing work, negotiating traffic, doing the childcare pick-up and getting home to get a dinner on the table they feel lucky if they have 15 minutes with their children before it is bedtime. I heard it often enough to embrace that 15-minute window and develop therapeutic, play-based parenting strategies that will make that 15 minutes work for you and your child in a way that will lead to *fewer tears and more laughter*.

As your children grow and develop, securing that 15-minute window to mindfully connect with them each day will prove more and more valuable – and *even the busiest young person can give their parents 15 minutes a day*, right?

Parenting is not an exact science and there are so many different and even conflicting schools of thought out there that getting it right or even mostly right most of the time can seem like an impossible goal. And just as you have it nailed, your children only go and grow up a stage so that what was working before no longer seems to. We need strategies that contain the flexibility to carry us through our children's various developmental stages; in other words, we need strategies that help us to grow up our parenting as our children grow and develop and this is why there are three books in my series, to carry you all the way from the *cradle to the rave*.

I really wanted to spotlight middle childhood, 8–12 years old, in this second book in my series because I believe it to be a very important, yet under-discussed stage of childhood development. We tend to focus on early childhood and then adolescence but overlook this vital middle stage, when so much is happening in your child's body, brain and their world to help them emerge from early childhood and prepare for adolescence.

In this book, I set out to give middle childhood the special space and focus it deserves. It tends to be a time when we stop actively playing with our children because it is also a time when their play patterns change significantly. Many will move away from more imaginative and creative play towards more structured and prop-focused play such as team sports, bikes, scooters, digital gaming and devices. What I wanted to create here, and hope that I have done so, is a road map to ensure that playful connection between you and your middle-childhood-aged child can be sustained throughout this time of intense physiological, neurological and psychological change.

I hope you loved my 15-Minute Parenting series and if you did I would be very grateful if you could write a review. I'd love to hear what you think, and it makes such a difference helping new readers to discover one of my books for the first time.

I love hearing from my readers – you can get in touch on my Facebook page, through Twitter, Goodreads or my website.

Thanks and remember... play is a state of mind and a way of being, regardless of age!

Joanna

JoannaFortuneSolamhClinic

@TheJoannaFortun

www.solamh.com

@joannafortune

Joanna Fortune

NOTES

1. Maunder, R. and Monks, C. P. (2019). Friendships in middle childhood: Links to peer and school identification, and general self-worth. *British Journal of Developmental Psychology* 37(2) pp.211–229.

2 Dunn, J. (2002). Sibling relationships. In Smith, P. K. and Hart, C. H. (eds), *Blackwell handbooks of developmental psychology. Blackwell handbook of childhood social development* (pp.223–237). Blackwell Publishing.

3 McHale, S. M. and Crouter, A. C. (1996). The family contexts of children's sibling relationships. In Brody, G. H. (ed.), *Advances in applied developmental psychology, 10. Sibling relationships: Their causes and consequences* (pp.173–195). Ablex Publishing.

4 Braiker, B. (26 September 2011). 'The next great American consumer: Infants to 3-year-olds.' *Adweek*.

5 Ito, T. A., Larsen, J. T., Smith, N. K. and Cacioppo, J. T. (1998). Negative information weighs more heavily on the brain: the negativity bias in evaluative categorizations. *Journal of Personality and Social Psychology* 75(4), pp.887–900.